One of the great challenges of being a Christian is learning to live into the freedom that Jesus offers us. In theory, it is an easy concept to grasp, but it's a difficult one to live out. Kevin Butcher so masterfully teaches us how we can take concrete steps toward that path. This book will leave you feeling inspired and empowered to break free from bondage as you fall into the loving arms of our Father.

PETER AHN, lead and founding pastor of Metro Community Church in Englewood, NJ

There is love that sets you free from the need to perform, achieve, strive, and earn. Such unapologetic love is found in Jesus. In the pages of *Free*, the veil between author J. Kevin Butcher's words and the love of Jesus is so thin; you will be overwhelmed, reader, by Butcher's nurturing invitation into your own belovedness. In these pages, your soul will be nourished and compelled to love God, others, and yes, even yourself freely.

AUBREY SAMPSON, church planter and pastor at Renewal Church, West Chicago, IL; speaker; and author of *The Louder Song* and *Overcomer*

Kevin is a master storyteller who beautifully articulates the transformative power of God's liberating covenant love. He helps move theology from the head to the heart and provides examples and pathways to genuinely live free.

ROBERT LEE, president and CEO of Pioneer Circuits

Defining a thing creates opportunities to see the thing through new lenses, strategize, and move accordingly. In this revelatory offering, Pastor Kevin unpacks the multilayered stronghold of shame while guiding us to the pathway to freedom. *Free* is an authentic, transparent conversation on the front porch with Kevin. It is heart-level communication from the Father, through Butcher, to his beloved. *Free* is an invitation to see, wrestle, and win. Each page creates space for the ah-has, tears, and screams necessary to move out of bondage and live FREE.

REV. WILLIAM MACK, pastor of Grace Community Covenant Church in Louisville, KY

Kevin Butcher understands better than anyone that Christians can drift from the love of Jesus into shaming religiosity. He writes about the love of Jesus so well that it's hard to believe that he, too, was rescued from the prison of performance Christianity. I was there. It's all true.

ED UNDERWOOD, president of Recentered Group, author of *When God Breaks Your Heart* and *Reborn to Be Wild*

I've met a lot of people who know a lot *about* Jesus. I don't know nearly as many who truly *know* Jesus. Kevin Butcher is most definitely the latter. Through this book, allow him to be your gentle, experienced guide away from "just do it" Christianity and a life of shame and into the freeing, healing embrace of Jesus' extravagant love.

ANGIE WARD, PHD, assistant director of DMin at Denver Seminary, author of *I Am a Leader*

This book is for those searching for more than just help in their spiritual growth. It is a practical guide for followers of Jesus who desire to enter the amazing freedom offered us in Christ. Kevin clearly describes this freedom and provides practical help in its pursuit. He reminds us that this freedom is found in embracing the love of Jesus and continually abiding in his love. You'll be helped and transformed as you read and apply what Kevin has explained for us all.

TOM YEAKLEY, author of *Growing Kingdom Character* and *Growing Kingdom Wisdom*

If you've never sat down and had a conversation with Kevin Butcher, you're about to. His deep love for God overflows and touches every person he meets, and that love flows through every word on the page. He's a passionate and skillful storyteller, and through this book, he graces us with a deeper experience of God's love. It's a timely message for those of us who've grown weary on the road of faith. Kevin speaks as one who doesn't just know *about* Jesus; he *knows* Jesus. And that is a gift to us all.

LEEANN SHAW YOUNGER, writer, speaker, cofounder and lead pastor of Cityview Church in Pittsburgh, PA

Kevin Butcher has penned a winner on how we practically experience and live out what it means to abide in Christ and his incredible love for us. This is not a dry theology book or another how-to book filled with suggestions for trying harder and being more disciplined. Butcher, with incredible authenticity, soaks us in the love of God for us that ignites a divine reaction in our hearts. Reading this book will be a spiritual experience for you.

BILL TELL, Navigator representative, author of *Lay It Down*

Too many of us are still trying too hard, still making too many commitments, and still starving on the same table scraps. Thank God for Kevin Butcher, who introduces us to a God who sets us free from religious performance by simply loving us.

STEVE WIENS, pastor at Genesis Covenant Church, Robbinsdale, MN; author of *Shining Like the Sun*

I have known Kevin for over thirty years. He is the real deal, and this book is the real deal. Every story and every point in this book is rooted in rugged and raw experience—doing real life with a real God. The shackles truly can be loosened, and freedom in Jesus can be a reality. This book will show you how.

JAMIE RASMUSSEN, senior pastor at Scottsdale Bible Church, Scottdale, AZ; author of *How Joyful People Think*

Kevin Butcher's passion for God and his word led him, through his own journey of faith, to discover the beating heart of God's unconditional love for each one of us. *Free* is a spring of fresh water that falls on the parched ground of rules-based Christianity. It will quench the thirst of everyone who has believed the lie that they must earn God's love. Theologically and historically grounded in Scripture, Kevin, with gut-honest truth, shares his own journey, as a follower of Jesus and pastor, into the freedom that comes from intimacy with Christ. Kevin Butcher has written a book about God's love that is a love letter to the church.

PAMELA E. PANGBORN, DMIN, pastor of Hope Community Church in Detroit, MI

When I was twenty, Kevin Butcher led me out of a "just do it" brand of Christianity and into a real relationship with Jesus. For thirty-six years, Kevin has passionately and faithfully pointed me back to Jesus, again and again. His transparent journey and personal insights into the surrendered life of living in Jesus' love, described in these pages, will point *you* back to Jesus for the freedom and life he longs for you to experience. Back to Jesus' deep heart of love for you and his beautiful invitation to abide in that love. Kevin's insights and personal journey are like a treasure map from a trusted guide.

MIKE FANNING, pastor of Idaville First Church of God, Idaville, IN

In a world shackled with shame, chained to contempt, and held hostage by hatred and guilt, we need to be *Free*. We all need the truths of this book! Butcher has a profoundly simple—yet simply profound—way of sharing the power of God's love and the freedom that comes when we wholeheartedly embrace it! If I could pour the truths of this book into every human being I know, I would! Why? Because we all need to be *Free*!

REV. LAWRENCE C. GLASS, JR., pastor of El Bethel Baptist Church, Redford, MI

FREE

RESCUED FROM
SHAME-BASED RELIGION,
RELEASED INTO THE
LIFE-GIVING LOVE OF JESUS

F R E E

J. KEVIN BUTCHER

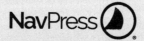

NavPress

A NavPress resource published in alliance
with Tyndale House Publishers

NavPress ◗

NavPress is the publishing ministry of The Navigators, an international Christian organization and leader in personal spiritual development. NavPress is committed to helping people grow spiritually and enjoy lives of meaning and hope through personal and group resources that are biblically rooted, culturally relevant, and highly practical.

For more information, visit NavPress.com.

for
Andrea
Leigh Anne
Caroline

Contents

Love (III)

Love bade me welcome; yet my soul drew back,
    Guilty of dust and sin.
But quick-eyed Love, observing me grow slack
    From my first entrance in,
Drew nearer to me, sweetly questioning
    If I lack'd anything.

"A guest," I answer'd, "worthy to be here":
    Love said, "You shall be he."
"I, the unkind, ungrateful? Ah, my dear,
    I cannot look on Thee."
Love took my hand, and smiling did reply,
    "Who made the eyes but I?"

"Truth, Lord; but I have marr'd them: let my shame
    Go where it doth deserve."
"And know you not," says Love, "who bore the blame?"
    "My dear, then I will serve."
"You must sit down," says Love, "and taste my meat."
    So I did sit and eat.

GEORGE HERBERT (1593–1633),
ANGLICAN CLERGYMAN

Introduction

YOU CAN'T STOP LOVE

It was 1959, the dead of winter in a small town in northern Indiana, and I was sitting on a rock-hard church pew alongside my parents for the Sunday-evening worship service. From my five-year-old viewpoint, the pastor seemed larger than life and a million miles away as he concluded his sermon with maybe the most famous verse in the New Testament:

> God so *loved* the world, that he gave his only Son, that
> whoever believes in him should not perish but have eternal life.
> JOHN 3:16, ESV, EMPHASIS ADDED

By that time in the service, other kids my age were either asleep or tearing pages out of the church hymnal. But I couldn't stop listening. As the pastor described the magnificent sacrificial love for each of us that compelled Jesus of Nazareth to embrace the Cross, I knew he was talking about Jesus going to that cross . . . for five-year-old me.

None of it makes sense, really. I was too young, the pastor too inaccessible, the description of the gospel too grown-up, too sophisticated, too religious—and why was my kindergarten self even paying attention to the old guy's sermon in the first place? David Crowder's lyric comes to mind: "You can't stop love."[1] On that blustery Indiana night, Jesus loved me enough to come and rescue me, to draw my tender heart—already wounded by the pain of life—to his compassionate arms.

My home was Christian—but full of broken people. I often felt unseen, misunderstood, and lonely. Shame already colored my view of myself; even at the age of five, I lived with an overwhelming sense of never being enough. But that evening, as I listened to the pastor talk about Jesus, I felt what the woman at the well must have felt, and Zacchaeus and the leper in Luke 5 when they first met the Savior—or Galilee's children when he picked them up and blessed them. I felt seen, accepted, embraced. Maybe for the first time ever, I felt emotionally safe. I felt enough.

So, as I listened to the pastor's final invitation to believe in Jesus, my little boy hand flew up and out of the pew. I felt like I was simply saying yes to the love I was thirsty for. Saying yes to home. I wasn't offered a choice between heaven and hell. I didn't know anything about the various historic views of the Atonement, or the meaning of words like *justification* or *redeemed*. All I remember is being compelled—by love.

So that winter evening sixty years ago, I met the most powerful, redemptive force in the universe: the sacrificial love of Jesus Christ. It was glorious, and even at the age of five, I knew I had to have more.

And then . . . I didn't. Sure, I'd get an occasional, fleeting glimpse of his love in the years to come. My first year at Taylor University, the Jesus-movement group Love Song was our homecoming enter- tainment, and I wanted the night to last forever because I felt five years old again as the band passionately sang "feel the love the Son of God can bring."[2] And yes, during those decades, I had some coaches, professors, friends—and eventually, an amazing wife—who not only followed Jesus but at times loved me and others well.

But here's the tragic reality: It was *over three decades* before I deeply and consistently experienced Jesus' love again.

Abide

What about you? If I asked, "Do you know, really know, that God loves you? Not just the world or your best friend—but *you?*" how would you respond? Some of us might immediately think of Bible verses to prove that we know God's love, but that's not the point. If I were to ask my grown daughter Andrea how she knows that I love her and hear that her only assurance was a card I sent her on her seventh birthday signed "love, Dad"—it would break my heart. Words alone can never take the place of a sustained, deep experience of love . . . not even inspired words from biblical text.

Or perhaps you're frustrated because you've felt the love of God, but very inconsistently. You assume a steadier life of walking in his love just isn't possible. Or if it is, you don't have a clue as to how to make it so. Maybe, dear friend, even now you're crying out from a lonely, broken place in your heart, *I want to believe there is something more to knowing Jesus than rules and trying harder. But I really wonder if Jesus' patient, unconditional love is available to someone . . . like* me?

You're not alone. So many of us who follow Jesus resist a "love of Jesus"-centered theology of the Christian life. Maybe we view God as our coach, and we're always trying to cut a tenth of a second off our "spiritual 40-yard dash time"; or we see him as our professor, so we're constantly cramming more spiritual information into our left brains; or we imagine him as our personal spiritual truant officer, scrutinizing our lives for misdemeanors and marching us off to spiritual jail.

But here is the great tragedy: Very few of us see God as our Healer, our Deliverer, our Father—deeply in love with us as his sons and daughters, calling us above all else to love him deeply in return. When we don't live in this "he really loves me" reality, our walk with Jesus is full of duty, fear, shame, and commands we find impossible to keep. The security, freedom, joy, and power of his transformative love is nowhere in sight. Many not only are discouraged but have simply checked out. They are dying. And I'm done standing by, watching them—watching you—die.

Not that I have this all figured out. Full disclosure: Before I started writing this book about living saturated in the love of God, I had to go back to Scripture one . . . more . . . time to ask, *Is the love of God really it? Is his love really the core spiritual substance that fills us, secures us, and launches us into battle against the powers of darkness? Is his love really the key to walking with Jesus? Not just for me, but for my struggling brothers and sisters, whom I love so dearly?*

In my search, I found myself once again in John 13–17, where Jesus, in his last pre-resurrection night on the planet, sends out his closest eleven followers with detailed instructions about what they need to carry on his work. As I read, one particular Jesus saying flew off the page:

As the Father loved Me, I also have loved you; *abide in My love.*

JOHN 15:9, EMPHASIS ADDED

I'd taught these words many times over the years, but *this* time they landed with fire in a place inside me where God speaks, and I know it's him. So I dug a little deeper, searching the most respected commentaries on John's Gospel for more perspective. One scholar's words almost took my breath away: He suggested that Jesus' call to "abide in My love" is "perhaps the nearest approach to an authoritative command in John to obey a . . . spiritual precept."[3]

In other words, out of all Jesus said to the disciples in John 13–17, and even John's entire Gospel, this is most important: *As you follow me, above all else you must abide in my love.*

The word *abide* is a favorite of John's, both in his Gospel and his letters, and means to "live, dwell, lodge"—sometimes with the connotation of remaining or continuing.[4] Jesus chose this word intentionally to call his disciples into an all-encompassing, comprehensive, intensely focused way of being with him and his love as they walked with him into their broken world and battled hell in his name. If Jesus stood before us today, issuing the same marching orders to us as spiritual descendants of his original eleven, he might say it like this:

My brothers and sisters, this is it—making your home in my love is how you walk with me and work with me to bring my healing Kingdom to our wounded world. Choose to dwell in my love, and even when hell is at your doorstep, my love will surround you, protect you, empower you, and set you free. Because my love isn't just important to your journey—*my love is everything.*

Weary follower of Jesus, are you getting this? It's not how much we study and work and try and confess and agonize and sweat. No— God's love is the *how* of the journey, the life we've been missing and

longing for. This love will cover, sustain, and free us to walk powerfully with him, no matter what the enemy brings. It's a love that will
lead us all the way home.

When my two oldest girls, Andrea and Leigh Anne, were small,
my wife Carla and I took them to a cabin on Lake Huron for a few
days of family time. The first afternoon, as we walked the beach,
Carla purposely lagged behind and secretly took a picture that I treasure. The sky is gray, a steep embankment covered by pine trees is on
our left, a bit of fog hovers over the water to our right, and straight
ahead, a seemingly endless stretch of rocky sand. Then, in the center
of the picture, walking together on the coastal pathway—me and my
two little girls. Andrea, in her yellow jacket, holding tightly to her
daddy's hand, and little three-year-old Leigh Anne, tiny arm fully
extended, barely reaching my fatherly grasp. It's an image you can
feel—my tenderness toward my girls, their confidence in my strength
and care. No fear. No need to perform. No worries about keeping up.
No thought of where they're going. All they know is a moment-by-
moment peace and freedom of walking with me, secure in my love.
*Exactly the kind of peace and freedom Jesus intends for us when he invites
us to make our home in his love.*

Listen: I'm deeply aware I don't have all the answers about what
it means to walk surrounded by Jesus' love. No one does. There's no
way for me to write anything close to comprehensive about how we
can live in a loving relationship with the all-knowing, all-powerful,
eternal Logos of God, who presently exists outside of time and space
and simultaneously says he is always with us. But what I *can* do
is share what I've personally learned—however imperfectly—about
abiding in his love from Scripture and church history in four decades
of study and teaching, along with what I've gleaned from the lives of
hundreds of Christ followers I've been privileged to walk with along

the way. Most importantly, I can vulnerably pour out *my* life—my broken, stumbling, empowering journey into the mystery of Jesus' powerful, healing love, that, after all my years of living in spiritual prison . . . is setting me free.

I get it that in Western Christianity, we don't like mystery. We prefer the concrete, the certain. Steps. Equations. Results. But intimate relationships are never like that. They are full of mystery. And frankly, I'm tired of cliché-filled, easy-answer, tightly packaged descriptions of our life with Jesus Christ—because none of these describe real relationship. Raw, authentic, unpredictable, elusive, powerful, intimate, overwhelming, irresistible, maddening, breathtaking—and yes, often deeply mysterious: These are the emotions I've come to experience in all my deepest relationships, including my daily sojourn with Jesus.

In life with Carla, I can point out certain things over the last forty-three years that have deepened our relationship. But I can't imagine telling her—ever—that what guides my journey with her is a list of ten directives I discipline myself to follow day after day in wooden, linear fashion! Intimacy doesn't follow a script. The closest of relationships are filled with images of affection, the aroma and fragrance of familiarity. And light—the light of deep and powerful love—pointing in a clear direction. In our life with God, we're not given a catalog of steps but a light and a love from a Father who never stops watching us with great affection, hovering over us with profound care and moving toward us with fatherly compassion and wisdom. Not because we've performed spiritually and won his approval—but simply because we are his beloved sons and daughters.

So, if on this journey into God's deep love, you want a more foolproof spiritual path—a step-by-step sheet of instructions like when you're building a set of boxed bookshelves for your den—or if you want a journey more guaranteed in terms of comfortable, cultural

Christian niceties along the way, you'll need to find another book to read. And, in truth, you'll need to find a different spirituality altogether. Because that's not the kind of path Jesus offers. Ever.

But he *does* offer a path. I'm praying that in the pages of this book, you will discern a mysterious yet well-lit *relational* pathway to Jesus' heart that is broad enough to include every kind of Jesus follower—male and female, old and young; every unique personality and nuanced ethnic background; every human experience of clarity and confusion, joy and sorrow. Because, hear this, son or daughter of God: *You and your story* are invited by Jesus himself into this mysterious, lifelong embrace of his love.

In fact, I believe our one great Love is with us right now. Not in some far-off galaxy but *here*, right beside me in the coffee shop where I'm writing and beside you wherever you are reading, just across the veil . . . in glory. He's with us and he loves us and he's waiting. His powerful, all-embracing hand of love is extended over history, his voice still echoing from that last moment with his eleven closest followers. And his invitation—his call on our lives—is still the same: *Abide. Abide in my love.*

The Barrier to Abiding

But because abiding in the love of Jesus is not only freeing but also spiritually powerful, we can expect pushback from the powers of darkness. Tragically, sometimes this persistent, insidious pushback comes through the message of the church. In fact, too often, followers of Jesus find themselves living under the life-sucking power of what shapes our Christianity when the love of Jesus isn't everywhere and everything: an ever-present, seemingly infinite list of religious rules.

When I was a teenager, my church friends and I were told over and over to "abstain from all appearance of evil" (1 Thessalonians 5:22, KJV). These words of Paul, always shared out of proportion and context, were accompanied by many devotionals and sermons on how to grit our spiritual teeth and discipline ourselves to obey a stern God who was constantly warning us with a shameful glare that if we didn't keep the rules, we weren't really "saved." We were told, "Repent harder, and pray the sinner's prayer again!" And again. And again. One normal, adolescent thought about sex, or an accidental swear word on the baseball field—and apparently, in God's eyes, we were done. Jesus, too, always seemed at least mildly angry with us. No matter what we did for him, it was never quite enough. In all honesty, I felt hopeless and absolutely hated being a Christian—feelings I wasn't supposed to have and was afraid to share. But even if I'd have had the courage to open up . . . there was no one to tell.

After high school and years of a steady training table of rules, many of my friends said, "I'm done" and walked away from Christianity altogether. I, however, dutifully chose to stick around and simply did my disciplined best to cope with a death-dealing lifestyle of shame. Over the next two decades, the rules themselves changed a bit—the list became less about never having a beer and more about rigorous adherence to the spiritual disciplines or never missing a chance to share my faith—but the point was still . . . the rules.

I call this kind of religion "just do it" Christianity—the veiled heresy that following Jesus is simply about Bible knowledge and trying really hard. In other words, as long as we know what the Scripture says and how it applies to a difficult situation, temptation, or sin pattern, all we need to do is step up to the plate, with Jesus as our cheerleader—and "just do it."

But this brand of Christianity has never worked and never will. In fact, the illusion of faith by sheer determination was exactly what led me to despair and near suicide as a young pastor. It is also this hellish, counterfeit variant of the Christian faith that I have watched, over the years, drain the life out of countless sincere believers, leaving them profoundly discouraged and disillusioned.

But, my brothers and sisters, it doesn't have to be this way. If you're absolutely wasted by "just do it" Christianity, sick of the grinding guilt and shame of walking an exhausting path of attempted spiritual discipline and obedience to an endless list of commands, if you long with an aching heart to give bleeding-out humanity a gospel powerful enough to heal their deepest relational wounds—Jesus Christ and his abiding love are available . . . and waiting. All you need is the courage to begin—or deepen—your own mysterious, empowering love relationship with the One who loves *you* with his everlasting love.

The Urgency of Abiding

Early one summer morning, as I sipped coffee on my back porch, I checked my phone for news and messages—and an avalanche of pain bled through the screen:

> > A precious, five-year-old daughter of God bludgeoned to death in a seedy urban Detroit hotel by her mother's boyfriend—plus two dozen marks of abuse discovered on her toddler brother . . .

> > A thirteen-year-old from a developing country, abandoned by her mother and alcoholic father, standing next to three younger siblings she was now responsible for feeding and protecting . . .

> > A text from a close friend, desperate and guilt-ridden about her broken daughter's third DUI and inevitable prison time . . .

Overwhelmed, I stopped reading . . . and wept. Of course, in my sixty-five years on the planet—and almost four decades as a pastor—I've seen and experienced plenty of pain. But this moment and these tears were different. I didn't just feel deep sadness but frustration and anger. Jesus of Nazareth, who preached and lived a powerful, sacrificial love that body-slammed death, calls all who follow him, above all else, to abide in that same powerful love (John 15:9). We who follow Jesus have the answer to the pain right in front of us—yet the pain seems to be mercilessly, continuously winning.

Do you feel this overwhelming pain—your own and the world's? Don't despair. This is the truth: Because of the healing power of Jesus' love, the enemy doesn't get to win. Yes, we're still surrounded by brokenness and death, but Satan's power is limited—he's not allowed to freely wander the planet pulling off his hellish agenda of murdering children, starving families, or breaking our spirits with depression, dysfunction, addiction, and abandonment. Why? Because the love of the Father that breathed life into Jesus' crucified body is available *to us* for our personal battle with the powers of darkness—and because *through us*, God promises to bring the full force of that same healing love of Jesus anytime Satan attacks God's sons and daughters, anywhere in the world. That is, if we choose to *abide*.

New Testament theologian N. T. Wright says it like this:

When Jesus died, the "powers" lost their power. They can still rage and shout, but the power of Jesus is stronger. . . . The past is blotted out. A new world has begun. A *revolution* has begun, in which power itself is redefined as the power of love. . . .

. . . Nothing in all creation can stop this all-powerful love.[5]

Abiding in the love of Jesus isn't optional. This is life or death—my life, your life, literally every precious life on the planet. Everything else—in our faith, our theology, our each-and-every-day experience—is secondary to our abiding experience of the love of God.

In fact, in a section of one of his letters, Paul decisively says, "[Even] if I have prophetic powers, and understand *all* mysteries and *all* knowledge, and if I have *all* faith . . . but have not love, *I am nothing*" (1 Corinthians 13:2, ESV, emphasis added). Only love—not knowledge and faith—he goes on to say, never ends and never fails. I can't stress this strongly enough: Armed with his love, we usher in the powerful, healing Kingdom of God . . . one battlefield, one relationship, one life at a time. Without knowing and experiencing God's love, we—and our broken world—have absolutely no hope.

This book is my attempt to point us toward our hope: a healer and deliverer named Jesus who offers us himself . . . and his all-encompassing love. It's about *how* to fall in love with Jesus—and then *how* to walk with Jesus, abiding in, surrounded by, protected by, and empowered by his love. You'll find nothing here about lists and shoulds. Our *how* begins with simply taking a step: accepting Jesus' invitation onto a relational pathway where we discover a love so powerful that it births our worship, obedience, and willingness to surrender all to him.

A few years ago, I got an e-mail from my close friend Gary—a successful and well-respected brother in our community—who had lived most of his life on the treadmill of performance and shame. He wrote,

> I had a breakthrough today. I finally get it that my sense
> of value has been skewed since I was a kid. I've worked my
> entire life to earn the approval of parents, coaches, friends,

customers, pastors—and God. As long as I was successful,
I was okay. I'm finally wrapping my heart around the
truth that I am a beloved son of the Father and am loved
regardless of what I do, whether I succeed or fail. I'm
beginning to experience joy and freedom I didn't know was
possible! I haven't arrived, but I'm on my way, and I want
even more![6]

This is a story I've heard over and over from those willing to make
the journey from "just do it" Christianity to falling in love with the
God who is in love with us. My brothers and sisters, this can be your
story too!

Know this: The words to follow don't come from a mountaintop
of arrival but from my own broken, sometimes halting experience of
(still) learning to live in love with Jesus, of beginning to see him as my
One Great Love. I pray that in reading, you are somehow encouraged
to begin to let go of the futility, bondage, discouragement, shame,
and despair of a religion that's only about trying harder. And that by
the last page, you might even feel you know *how* to begin receiving—
and keep choosing—freedom within the powerful, warm embrace of
the One who loves you more than life itself.

Chapter 1

OUR ONE GREAT LOVE

God is love, and he who abides in love abides in God, and God in him.

I JOHN 4:16

To fall in love with God is the greatest romance.

AUGUSTINE OF HIPPO

*All that is not the love of God has no meaning for me. . . . I have no
interest in anything but the love of God which is in Christ Jesus.*

DOMINIQUE VOILLAUME

**Abiding in Jesus' love is learning to
believe his love—is everything.**[*]

"I REMEMBER THE DAY I WAS CHOSEN," Nadia told me as we sat over
coffee one afternoon. Earlier that morning, I had shared with her
Bible-college class about Paul's tender image of God adopting us "as
his own children" (Romans 8:15, NLT). When I asked if anyone in
the room had been adopted, Nadia shyly raised her hand, and later
that day, she graciously recounted what adoption was like for her.

Nadia was born in an Eastern Bloc country, and her memories of the orphanage were bleak. Poor living conditions, abuse,

---

[*] Dominique Voillaume was a priest with the Little Brothers of Jesus. These were the last lines written in his diary
before he died. Dominique never wrote a book, preached to large crowds, or entertained dignitaries, but he walked
with God, abiding in Jesus' love and loving those around him, especially the poor, with that same powerful, healing
love. Seven thousand people attended his funeral.

loneliness—and worst of all, hopelessness. Nadia told me, "I didn't really understand the adoption process, but I knew how it felt to watch other children get chosen to leave the orphanage—and then walk back to my room . . . alone."

One day, when she was nine years old, Nadia was given a rare shower—"really only a few drops of water." And then, her first dress ever. Finally, Nadia was taken into a room where a smiling man and woman waited for her. They ushered her to a waiting automobile—and quickly the newly formed trio was off to the airport for a long flight across Europe and the Atlantic Ocean to the US. Then Nadia found herself in another car, and eventually she arrived at a home larger and nicer than anything she had ever seen.

"To be honest, the whole time, I wasn't completely sure what was happening," she told me. "I'd rarely been in a car, never on a plane—and my grown-ups only spoke English. But everything became clear when after a bath, they tucked me in my own bed with a new pair of pajamas and fresh, crisp sheets. Then, the nice man leaned over and whispered—somehow in a way I could understand—'From now on, sweetheart, call me Daddy.' Pastor Kevin, at that moment I knew . . . I was home."

This must have been what Paul wanted his readers to "feel":

You have not received a spirit that makes you fearful slaves. Instead, you received God's Spirit when he adopted you as his own children. Now we call him, "Abba, Father."
ROMANS 8:15, NLT

Listen carefully: We aren't God's slaves—we're his beloved sons and daughters. And not by accident. He walked into the cosmic orphanage one day and *chose* us to be his children. Despite our baggage, brokenness, and sin, he longed for us to be his own. Sometimes in my shame, I envision someone pulling God off to the side, pointing at me, and warning, "Uh, God, you really don't want *this* one—let me tell you why." But the truth is, he already knows all about me—not just my strengths and potential but also every unattractive detail and weakness. He knows about you, too. And yet, he chose—and chooses—us still. Because he's our Father and he loves us.

In fact, in his letter to the Roman church, Paul intentionally uses an Aramaic term that implies even deeper intimacy: *Abba*. On the streets of Jerusalem, if you're near a young Israeli family, you'll hear the small children crying out, "Abba, Abba" if and when they call for their daddy. *Abba* is also the term Jesus used to address his Father in Gethsemane on the toughest night of his earthly life, when he felt alone and afraid (Mark 14:36).

When my girls were growing up, I was their pastor, their mother's husband, co-owner of the home they lived in, and sometimes their coach . . . but our relationship flourished only when they could see me as their father—when they were secure enough in my love to call me *Daddy*. In the same way, Nadia finally understood her new life when she realized that the man who took her from the orphanage was now her loving father. Dear friends, please don't miss this—we will only experience freedom in our relationship with God when we let go of our pressurized, shaming images of him and realize he's our Father who chose us and adopted us because he loves us, that even though he's our Creator, Lord, and King, he invites us to call him "Abba."

Many of us feel more comfortable imagining the face of Jesus than God the Father. Recently, during a particularly difficult moment in her spiritual journey, Carla asked me, "Can I believe in Jesus and not believe in God?" This is a dilemma many of us face: "Jesus feels close and full of empathy. God sometimes feels distant and uncaring."

But hear Jesus' words one more time: "As the Father has loved me, so have I loved you" (John 15:9, ESV). Clearly, in the way they love us, the Father and the Son are inseparable. When Jesus invites us to "abide in my love," he could have easily said, "abide in our love." For sure, there is Trinitarian mystery here, but practically speaking, the Father and the Son love us in tandem. As we move into the abiding life, we'll find ourselves understanding and experiencing the love of both in deeper ways than ever before!

What if you woke each morning to the kind and gentle gaze of your loving Father? He's been sitting on the edge of your bed, waiting for you to wake up, watching over you with love and delight. What if the first words you heard as you began your day were these words of Jesus: "I've loved you the way my Father has loved me. Make yourselves at home in my love. If you keep my commands, you'll remain *intimately* at home in my love. . . . I've told you these things for a purpose: that my joy might be your joy" (John 15:9-15, MSG, emphasis added)? Imagine starting each day with this truth from the mouth of Jesus Christ himself, an invitation to step into a rhythm of life where our focus isn't obedience but instead his love—which inspires obedience filled with joy! Drudgery, dread, and bondage would immediately be replaced by excitement, anticipation, and freedom.

Some of you may remember Sophia from *Choose and Choose Again*. Many years ago, she found herself on the streets of Detroit—lonely, abused, saturated with shame, desperately trying to fill her emptiness and numb her pain through drugs and prostitution.[1] When she finally realized that the love of Jesus was everything she was looking for, she walked away from decades of darkness.

A few weeks ago, I got this text from Sophia—who today has her GED, is employed, and is restoring her relationships with the children that she abandoned during her empty years: "Pastor Butcher,

Jesus Christ continues to reign in my life!! His love is the foundation on which I stand!!! He is the Alpha and the Omega and is still sooo much alive in me!!! Hallelujah!" Every exclamation point jubilantly shouts the passionate love and joy that feeds her relationship with Jesus.

But for many of us, this kind of love-filled, joy-saturated life is far removed from our experience. Instead, the first thing we "see" when we get up in the morning is a list of imposing rules staring at us, immediately and threateningly demanding our obedience. Some of the rules are human-made churchy legalisms, for sure. But much of the list is essentially good—commands given from the heart of a loving God, pointing to a pathway that leads to life. Yet in John 15:9, Jesus doesn't call us to begin with God's good and life-giving commands. Instead, he instructs us to first receive and make our home in his love. Jesus is clear: *Passionate obedience flows out of living in love*—and ironically, that very obedience leads us to a deeper abiding (John 15:10)!

Unfortunately, that's not what most of us—even veteran followers of Jesus, lifelong churchgoers, serious Bible students, Sunday-school teachers, and church leaders—believe to be true. We may say we believe it, but our lives speak a different reality. Many of us haven't even heard this truth before. I don't recall much talk about God's love in seminary. When we studied Ephesians line by line, my gifted professors appropriately emphasized "by grace you have been saved through faith" (Ephesians 2:8)—but not so much "God chose us in Christ . . . in *love*" (Ephesians 1:4, author's paraphrase) or "because of His great *love* with which He *loved* us" (Ephesians 2:4) or "that you, being rooted and grounded in *love*" (Ephesians 3:17) or "as *beloved* children . . . walk in *love*" (Ephesians 5:1-2, ESV; all emphasis added). Yes, God's grace is of paramount importance because it's how he gives us life. But God's love motivates his grace—he is gracious to us because he loves us. God's love is his heart, his soul. His love is virtually ground zero of everything he feels about us and does for us. God's love isn't just another of his attributes. My friends, *God is love* (1 John 4:16).

One evening when Carla was out, I decided to sort through some mementos from our girls when they were young. Big mistake—especially alone! I pulled out a tiny note my then-seven-year-old Leigh Anne had written me years earlier—in sky-blue letters surrounded by sky-blue hearts: "I love Mi Daddy, from Leigh Anne." Of course, I dad-cried and immediately texted my grown-up daughter, who tenderly replied, "I've always just wanted to be your little girl, much like my heart really just longs to be God's precious daughter. What a great parallel. I love you, Dad." Leigh Anne has two degrees, is an accomplished therapist, and has an incredibly full life. But her moment-by-moment core reality as a professional woman, wife, mom, and human being is the love of a God who calls himself her Father. A love mirrored in my love for her and reflected in every love she experiences. Are you feeling this? God's love was never designed to be a sidebar concern. His love is meant to be . . . everything.

This truth about the centrality of God's love explains so much about Jesus' emphasis on abiding in his love. The context of his words in John 15 is crucial. On the night before his death (John 13) Jesus had the rapt attention of his eleven closest followers. He had just explained that he was leaving, that they couldn't follow—and that from now on they would *be him* in the broken, hostile world around them. The disciples anxiously hung on every word as they waited for Jesus to tell them what was next, what to do, how to survive, how to continue his Kingdom mission . . . and it's in this decisive, pivotal moment that Jesus commanded, "Abide in My love" (John 15:9).

Because the bottom line is this—the love of God in Jesus Christ is the soil from which *everything* in God's Kingdom germinates, grows, and flourishes. When we choose to replace that love with try-harder, shame-based religion, his Kingdom shrivels and dies because we're no longer rooted in the source of all life. Christianity's emphasis on the "rules"—what Greg Boyd calls our post–Genesis 3 obsession with "good and evil"[2]—and the corresponding dismissal of Jesus' abiding love as relatively insignificant, are lies from hell that are killing us *and* our healing, redemptive impact on the world.

Listen: The reason we can't conquer racism isn't because we don't have enough seminars or dialogues on race but because we don't believe his love is everything—a powerful love that topples racist societal structures, moves perpetrators to repent, and compels the wounded to forgive. One reason broken relationships in the church look so much like those in our culture isn't because we don't have enough books or small groups about healing marriages and pursuing reconciliation in our families but because we don't believe his love is everything—a covenant love that sacrifices for the other even when others have nothing left to give. The reason we don't see more hurting human beings come to faith in Jesus Christ isn't because we haven't found the perfect evangelism strategy but because we don't believe his love is everything—a compassionate, pursuing love that moves us toward those who don't yet believe, a compelling love that can overwhelm the defenses of the most ardent skeptic and draw them home to the Father.

For certain, a rules-based, love-starved faith almost killed me. By the time I was thirty-six, three decades removed from my first encounter with the love of God, my life dripped the poison of years of immersion in hell's counterfeit, rule-saturated version of walking with Jesus. It was the only Christianity I knew. In 1990, I had been pastoring seven years and found myself leading my second church while embracing the latest version of "the list"—preaching perfect sermons, trying to make everyone happy, working ungodly long hours—while secretly petrified of failure and always thinking I should have done more. I was successful, married to my best friend, the father of three incredible daughters . . . and yet, experiencing precious little of the Father's love. I was an empty shell inside—a dead man walking.

I'm convinced my story is not an isolated one. Perhaps you, too, are feeling dead inside, reeling from the impact of a false Christianity's focus on rules and relegation of God's love to secondary status. Perhaps you're empty and spiritually exhausted from long days of sweating and trying and striving to please a God who seems impossible to please. Maybe you're near tears as you read these words and sense your deep longing for intimacy with the One who, from the beginning, has presented himself to us as our One Great Love. What if you could begin to let go of all the false images of God as a demanding tyrant—and begin to believe he's a good Father who deeply loves . . . you?

As a lifelong Cubs fan, I'll never forget the day I first took my three girls to Wrigley Field. The look of wonder on their faces as they experienced the sights and sounds of a major-league ballpark was priceless. Before we found our seats, I led them to the nearest concession stand, knelt next to them, arm around all three as they huddled near me, and pointed to the neon menu. "Girls," I said, "do you see what I see? Popcorn, hot dogs, ice-cream sandwiches, lemon ice, Cracker Jack, cotton candy! Today, whatever you want—it's yours!" Then, I pointed to the souvenir stand a few feet away, filled with Cubs T-shirts, baseball hats, autographed balls, key chains, pennants, and bobble heads. "Ladies, before we go home today, whatever you like—it's yours!" All three nodded their heads rapidly, eyes wide as saucers, as if thinking, *Can this be happening? Can our daddy really love us this much?* Recently, I asked the girls if they remembered this childhood moment—and they did—but Leigh Anne articulated a feeling that seemed to express what they all felt: "Of course I remember, Dad. But the truth is, it wasn't just the Cubs game. I remember lots of moments of you doing that exact same thing at lots of different places. *That's just how you always were with us.*"

Remember Jesus' story of the Prodigal Son, who comes home after years of partying, determined to tell his dad how sorry he is and how he no longer deserves to be his son? But when his dad sees him coming down the road, he runs to meet him, compassionately hugs and kisses him, and lavishes him with gifts, including a welcome-home party! And then, the father also pursues the rule-keeping older brother, tenderly reminding him, "Dear son . . . everything I have is yours" (Luke 15:31, NLT). Do you see it? The father in the story represents the God who is *our* Father, and he's not about *demanding from us*—but lavishly and compassionately *giving to us.* Because he loves us. Worn-out brother or sister, that's how he always is with us. That's how he always is . . . with you.

One thing I know is that everywhere I describe *this kind of love* and how central it is, with an audience of thousands or a brother or sister over coffee—the response is always the same. "Why haven't I heard this before? How could I go to church all these years and come away knowing everything about the rules—but knowing so little of God's extravagant love? No wonder I'm desperate and empty inside. No wonder most days, I just want to be done." And then, the tears begin to fall.

Here's the difficult truth: The church has "left [its] first love" (Revelation 2:4). We've traded our relational birthright of living freely, powerfully, and redemptively as God's beloved sons and daughters for a porridge chock-full of rules. We've pawned the pearl of great price—the precious, personal, abiding love of Jesus—for a few religious coins. Most of us haven't heard that God's love is everything because to so many of us, even those in church leadership, it is not. Over fifty years ago, renowned continental theologian Hans Urs von Balthasar wrote that if the church didn't begin to live as if God's love was central, our world had "scarcely any chance left of encountering the heart of Christianity."[3] I'm worried that what he prophesied is here.

So, what to do? Most importantly, *we must reject the satanic lie that Jesus' love is somehow secondary—and choose to embrace the truth that his love is everything.* Because you can be sure of this: If we think anything else is more foundational than his love—*that* space is where we will make our home. When we do that, the enemy will have us right where he wants us, saturating our lives in good things, even spiritual things, while we miss the power of the main thing—the love of God in Jesus Christ.

A key turning point for me—a moment when I began to own his love as everything—was when I discovered that the centrality of God's love in Christ isn't about what I say or what anyone else says. It's about what the Bible has always clearly said:

> > *Genesis*: In the very beginning, God presents himself as our One Great Love, creating Adam and Eve "by the fire of love"[4] and then walking intimately, daily[5] with them in the Garden (Genesis 3:8).

> > *Deuteronomy*: God's love is central when he tells Israel he chose her simply because he loves her (Deuteronomy 4:37; 7:7-8) and

then calls his people first and foremost to "love the LORD [their] God with all [their] heart[s]" in return (Deuteronomy 6:5-6).

> *Psalms*: God's love is the heart of David's cry, "Give thanks to the LORD, for . . . His faithful love endures forever" (Psalm 107:1, NLT).

> *Song of Solomon*: We hear echoes of God's love for us and our love for him in the passionate utterances of a young Shulamite bride: "I am my beloved's, and my beloved is mine"; "his banner over me was love" (Song of Solomon 6:3; 2:4).

> *Isaiah*: God's love permeates his promise to Zion: "I will not forget you. . . . I have inscribed you on the palms of My hands" (Isaiah 49:15-16).

> *Hosea*: God calls the prophet to love an unfaithful, struggling prostitute to prove to Israel that even when she forgets him, "I will betroth you to me forever . . . in steadfast love" (Hosea 2:19-20, ESV).

> *Romans*: Paul proclaims love as the heart of our identity in Christ, declaring that nothing "shall be able to separate us from the love of God which is in Christ Jesus our Lord" (Romans 8:38-39).

> *Galatians*: Love is crucial to what some describe as Paul's life verse: "the life which I now live in the flesh I live by faith in the Son of God, who loved me and gave Himself for me" (Galatians 2:20).

> *1 Peter*: God's love informs Peter's core understanding of our life with Jesus—"whom having not seen [we] love" (1 Peter 1:8).

> *1 John*: The beloved disciple declares that love is God's very essence: "God is love, and whoever abides in love abides in God, and God abides in him" (1 John 4:16, ESV).

> *Jude*: God's love is central to Jude's instruction for spiritual battle: "Keep yourselves in the love of God" (Jude 1:21).

> *Revelation*: John's mystical vision is dedicated "to Him who loved us and washed us from our sins in His own blood" (Revelation 1:5).

And nowhere in the biblical narrative is the love of God more central than in the story of the Cross: "God so *loved* the world, that he gave his only Son" (John 3:16, ESV, emphasis added). Bishop Kallistos Ware says it powerfully:

> "It is finished" . . . is to be understood, not as a cry
> of resignation or despair, but as a cry of victory: It is
> completed, it is accomplished, it is fulfilled.
>   What has been fulfilled? . . . The work of suffering love,
> the victory of love over hatred. Christ our God has loved his
> own to the uttermost.[6]

No wonder Jesus, at the end of his life, calls his disciples—and us—to "abide in [his] love." He knew beyond doubt that this intimate relationship with our God—our husband, our Abba, our One Great Love—was intended to be the lifeblood of our journey with him. Jesus, the eternal Logos of God, knew that his love . . . is everything.

A few years back, I led a men's retreat in northern Arizona. After the Friday evening session, Derek approached me, and a few moments into our conversation, it was clear we had much in common—walking alongside our wives as they battled cancer, a deep passion to be good fathers, and the ever-present struggle to become better men. Derek was gifted, articulate, and easy to talk with, so by the time we walked to the dining hall for late-night pizza, our hearts were genuinely connecting. At the end of the evening, I placed my hands on Derek's shoulders, looked at him with my father eyes, and tenderly said, "I love you, son." I embraced him, then made my way back to my room. Derek didn't say much in the moment, but sometime later, he sent me a text: "Hey Kev, I wanted you to know that while I've said 'I love you, son' a thousand times to my boys over the years, I didn't realize how much I longed to hear those words said to me."

Right now, I'm thinking about each of you, with tears. My sisters and brothers, fellow weary travelers, struggling with difficult life circumstances and a Christianity that offers you nothing more for the journey than a bundle of religious rules and a shaming voice whispering, *Try harder*. But here's what I'm praying you're beginning to understand: God isn't shame-based Christianity. God is your Father. He chose you, he still chooses you—and right now, his strong, tender hands are on *your* shoulders, he's gazing into *your* eyes, and speaking words *your* heart has been longing to hear: "I love you, son. I will always love you, daughter. From now on, call me Abba."

United Pursuit sings, "I'm laying down all my religion . . . I want to know you, Lord."[7] What are you hanging on to, focusing on, or abiding in that is keeping you from taking an all-embracing step toward the abiding love of God in Jesus Christ? Are you ready to lay it down in order to know him and abide in him? Are you ready to choose the joy, the power, and the freedom of walking with him as your One Great Love? The Jesus of John 15:9 is very near. His loving hands are open, and his strong-yet-gentle voice is calling: "Abide. Abide in my love."

Chapter 2

DESPERATION

As the deer pants for the water . . .
So pants my soul for You, O God.
My soul thirsts for God, for the living God.

PSALM 42:1-2

God desires to be [our] thirst.

HADEWIJCH OF ANTWERP,

THIRTEENTH-CENTURY FLEMISH MYSTIC

Love is not merely a warmth to bask in . . . but a grave,
fierce yearning and reaching out for Paradise itself.

FREDERICK BUECHNER

Abiding in Jesus' love calls us
to live with desperation for him.

A FEW MONTHS AGO, as I was cleaning out some boxes, I found a
worn index card covered with my middle daughter Leigh Anne's
handwriting. She had written it a few years back when she was in
seminary, pursuing a degree in counseling and braving a hazardous,
frightening river called *Desperation*. One afternoon, lonely, confused,
and overwhelmed by a very personal "dark night," my grown-up little
girl penned this sacred, vulnerable prayer:

God, pull back the veil to reveal my other lovers. Show
me their shallowness and terminal insufficiency. Help me

to stop playing the victim, blaming you for my loneliness. Remind me of your story, *the* story, and help me choose to pursue you. Be my husband, drawing me into sweet, rich, deep intimacy with you. Please make this the constant cry of my heart.

Even today, it's hard for me to read these words. As a dad, I always want to protect my girls from pain and be their rescuing hero. But this time, Leigh Anne needed "a greater Father," an Abba who alone could come close and fill her heart with the peace, love, and intimacy she was longing for. That dark afternoon, she got honest and came face-to-face with her passionate longing for her One Great Love. In her desperation, she asked him to create even deeper desperation in her heart . . . for him. It was a turning point. She cried out—and began to abide.

Many years ago, after decades of a Christianity driven by rules and performance, I, too, found myself in a place of utter desperation. One evening, feeling like I was drowning, I came impulsively close to ending my life. The church I was pastoring at the time was difficult and discouraging, but there was no precipitating tragedy that moved me to near suicide. I was simply overwhelmed by the pain and emptiness of not knowing I was loved by the God I was diligently trying to serve. Up until that night, my relationship with God had been primarily about Bible content and the discipline to obey. It was routine, somewhat formal, respectful, a spiritual business arrangement of sorts—an "I've saved you, now I'll teach you how to save others, so obey me and all will be well" kind of Kingdom deal. But that night, everything changed. Driving along a freeway in Detroit, I came face to face with my deep longing for intimacy with him—an overwhelming need to live surrounded by his love. There was no going back. Either God was more than distant holiness, a list of good rules, and constant commands . . . or I was done. I would not, could not live that way anymore. I had arrived in the land of desperation.

The details of that night—including the way God saved my life—are in my book *Choose and Choose Again*. But from that moment forward, as God graciously began to reveal his profound love for me, I began pursuing him with the imperfect but desperate passion of a hero-worshiping son or a wildly star-crossed lover. Today, I abide in the love of Jesus not because I can but because I must. Yes, because I'm in love with him, but also because without his love, I don't just struggle; I begin to devolve. Without the safety, power, and comfort of his love, my personal version of the flesh—shame, anger, a bullying spirit, jaded skepticism, and emotional darkness—begins to creep in. For me, intimacy with God and his Son, Jesus, isn't an option, a casual choice I can make if I'm in the right spiritual mood. Without connecting daily, moment by moment with Jesus and his love for me, I'm literally undone. For me, *abiding isn't primarily about discipline but desperation.*

This doesn't mean being disciplined isn't a component of my relationship with Jesus. Of course it is, just as it's a part of my relationship with Carla. For example, even though she's my wife and best friend, it takes a degree of discipline for me to pull back from a packed schedule to intentionally set aside time to be with her. But make no mistake, what moves me to take that small, disciplined step—and many others—is the fact that I'm passionately, desperately in love with her. It's the longing, the heartfelt, intense desire—the desperation—that has kept us moving toward one another for forty-three years, through the spiritual battle of raising children; the all-too-often lunacy of pastoral ministry; financial struggles; our personal journeys with temptation, sin, and forgiveness; and numerous health issues. Let me say it even more boldly: There's not enough discipline in the world that could have kept us together had it not been for our deep and desperate love for one another. A desperate love fueled and empowered, of course, by our desperate love for our Christ, who first and always desperately loves us.

The truth is, no one longs for bland, casual, disciplined relationships that continue to exist just because "we promised." Sure, disciplined commitment will certainly help us soldier on through difficult times. But we want spouses, parents, kids, family, and friends who miss us terribly when we're gone and greet us with deep, heartfelt smiles and passionate embraces when we return. Desperation and passion produce relationships that flourish, endure, and bring us the deepest joy.

After counseling hundreds of couples and other struggling friends, I promise you—relationships void of desperation simply don't last. They may look healthy enough on the surface, but deep in the inner corridors of the relationship itself, where there used to be a vibrant, passionate, desperate heart, the deafening silence betrays the truth. Though the couple or friends may stay together out of sheer commitment, the relationship itself is all but dead.

That's exactly how it is in our relationship with Jesus. Discipline can only take us so far. Without desperate, passionate longing for him—which keeps us leaning into and abiding in his love—something between us begins to die. Because of the Cross and forgiveness, we're still his, but the relationship itself goes on autopilot. It begins to atrophy, becoming a shell of its former self. Then one day, we realize our relationship with God is mere formality, almost as if we have no relationship at all.

It was never meant to be this way. In Scripture, we see this kind of passion and desperation at the heart of relationship with

God—*everywhere.* Possibly the most famous Old Testament picture of desperate passion for the Lord is the oft-referenced scene in 2 Samuel 6 where King David "danced with great abandon" before the Ark of the Covenant in the sacred processional that delivered the Ark to Jerusalem (2 Samuel 6:12-16, MSG). David's desperate display of deep love for his God is so blatant, so emotionally overwhelming— even for the passionate worshiping culture of Israel—that his wife Michal rebukes him for "exposing himself to the eyes of the servants' maids like some burlesque street dancer!" (2 Samuel 6:20-22, MSG).

Over and over, too, in the Psalms, David describes his pursuit of God in the desperate language of a choice between life and death. In Psalm 42:1, he passionately sings, "As the deer pants for the water brooks, so pants my soul for You, O God." Or in Psalm 84:2: "My soul longs, yes, even faints for the courts of the LORD; my heart and my flesh cry out for the living God." In these two psalms and many others, David isn't subtle or nuanced. His relationship with God isn't motivated by convenience or habit. David is desperate. He's in frantic, frenzied, life-or-death pursuit. Even as a king with all the resources of the ancient Near East at his disposal, David knows the only place to find life-saving, sustaining nourishment: God's "constant love," which is "better than life itself" (Psalm 63:3, GNT). In David's mind, if he doesn't live his life passionately and intimately connected to that love, he's as good as dead.

In Jesus, God brings his healing love bodily to earth and connects with our pain up close and personal, which is why the New Testament is full of people desperately seeking him. In Luke 7, we meet a woman whom Luke simply calls "a sinner"—probably a local "woman of the night." We don't know her background, her circumstances, or how she got involved with her trade. But we can feel her pain and desperation, this one who, for some years, has been serially used and mortally wounded in her soul. When she hears that Jesus of Nazareth is dining in the home of Simon the Pharisee, she breaks all protocol by bursting (uninvited) through the door of Simon's home and falling, sobbing, at Jesus' feet. Without shame, she spontaneously bathes the feet of the God-man with her many tears, using her hair to massage them clean, then completes her fervent worship by anointing them with costly perfume (Luke 7:38). Why did this daughter of God, so abused by men, so fiercely seek the affection and comfort of *this man*? My guess is that she'd recently seen Jesus radically love a bleeding-out, marginalized someone on a Galilean street or listened to him compassionately speak the love of God to broken thousands on a hillside and instantly knew, *This man isn't like other men. He would never hurt me or use me because he truly, desperately loves . . . even me.* And so, this forgiven daughter desperately loves Jesus in return.

There's more. Lepers were considered spiritually unclean and forced to stay separated from Jewish society. But in Mark's Gospel, we learn of a leper who is so desperate to see Jesus, and so convinced Jesus will love and accept him, that he walks right up to Jesus, falls at his feet, and begs for healing (Mark 1:40). A woman who had suffered for twelve years with "constant bleeding"—and spent all her money on pursuing a cure—braves a crowd mobbing Jesus just to touch "the fringe of his robe" (Luke 8:43-44, NLT). Short-statured Zacchaeus, a tax collector marginalized in both Roman and Jewish society, fights his way through a Jericho throng and climbs a tree, hoping for even a fleeting glimpse of Jesus (Luke 19:1-4). After an all-night fishing expedition, Peter launches his post-denial, guilt-ridden body into the Sea of Galilee, desperate to get to his beloved Jesus, whom he's just seen on the shore (John 21:7).

Paul, a former murderer, was so desperate to intimately know Jesus Christ that he counted "everything else . . . worthless" by comparison

(Philippians 3:8, NLT). Over and over in his letters, Paul makes it crystal clear that Jesus was never meant to be a casual part of our life—he literally "*is* our life" (Colossians 3:4, emphasis added). To Paul, God is our Father—the opposite of distant, casual, or stoic—whose love compels us to passionately "cry out, 'Abba'" when we approach him (Romans 8:15).

Without fail, Scripture describes our walk with God—abiding in Jesus' love—as *inseparably linked to passionate desperation*. Should we be surprised, then, that over the years, so many enduring voices in the history of Christianity have spoken boldly of their desperate longing for God's love? Theologian Augustine of Hippo (AD 354–430) said, "To fall in love with God is the greatest romance"—words that mirrored his own journey from despair to the Father's heart.[1] Medieval mystic Catherine of Siena (AD 1347–1380), who described God as "a fire of love,"[2] closed every letter with the spiritually amorous words, "sweet Jesus, Jesus Love."

Look, it would be tempting to think that these biblical characters and other historic followers of Jesus are in some special category. But no—they are men and women like you and me, with the same hopes, fears, challenges, joys, and sorrows. What sets them apart is that the essence of their relationship with God was never about biblical commands or spiritual disciplines; it was about their desperate, passionate love for him. In the early twentieth century, a young Chinese village girl, commanded by Communist soldiers to "trample the cross and live," instead lifted her hands heavenward and sang "Jesus Loves Me"—as their guns blazed, sending her to glory.[3] We'll do a lot for someone we believe in. We'll sacrifice everything for someone we desperately love.

In recent months, I've been deeply moved by author Mary DeMuth's memoir *Thin Places*, where she details the trauma of her childhood sexual abuse and the years of recovery that followed. As she reflects on how she survived such horrific, painful betrayal, she decides to read her adolescent diaries for clues to her spiritual perseverance and grit:

> As I read these journals I see something startling: my heart. Bleeding all over those journals twenty years younger, a pattern emerges. *I am insanely in love with Jesus Christ.* I trip up . . . but even in my straying, He's constantly on my mind. Pen to paper, I shower Him with affectionate words. I scribble His messages to me. I devour the Bible and memorize its beauty. God sees me, and I also see Him. And love Him.[4]

"I am insanely in love with Jesus Christ." Those words leap at lightning speed into my father heart, bringing tears because of Mary's little-girl pain and the unspeakable violation she endured—and hope because her words reflect a desperation for Jesus and his invincible, conquering love, even when the enemy is at his diabolical worst. A desperation necessary for anyone in any era to consistently abide.

Because the reality is—please don't miss this—*we're created in the image of a passionate God to long for and search for something or someone to be profoundly, desperately passionate about!* Or, as George McDonald put it in a nineteenth-century sermon, "The soul God made is . . . hungering."[5] If we're not desperate for him, we *will* be desperate for something else. Casually following God won't cut it. Eventually the bright lights and compelling promises of other lovers will lure us away like Disney's Pinocchio, who meant so well but still ended up on Pleasure Island, braying like the donkey he had become. Some years ago, the prolific Porphyrios said it this way: "When people are empty of Christ, a thousand and one other things come and fill them up; jealousies, hatreds, boredom, melancholy, resentment, a worldly outlook, worldly pleasures."[6] Invitations to passion, all.

Think about it—King David stepped away for just a moment from his desperate pursuit of God . . . and quickly moved toward the passion of adultery, calculated betrayal, and murder. Or consider Demas, a serious Jesus follower and one of Paul's closest companions (Colossians 4:14; Philemon 24)—of whom Paul says in his last letter, as he awaits Roman execution, "Demas has deserted me *for love of this present world*" (2 Timothy 4:10, author's paraphrase). He could have said, "Demas stopped reading his Bible and lost his faith" or "Demas wasn't disciplined enough, so he couldn't handle the pressure." But instead, Paul uses language of passion—Demas left because he *loved* the world. We can only guess the details, but it's clear that in Paul's mind, for a long while, Demas was in love with Jesus. At some point, for whatever reason, Demas's passion waned, and very soon his empty heart found another lover: the world and what it promised him. Then, when the spiritual battle got too intense, he walked away.

The truth is, without desperation in our love relationship with God, everyone eventually walks away. We might walk ten steps into lukewarm complacency, a hundred yards into discouragement, or five miles into apostasy—but I promise, everyone walks. And absolutely no one continues to abide.

So, if desperation is essential to abiding in Jesus' love, how do we get desperate and stay desperate for him? I'm a little afraid of sounding cliché, theologically unsophisticated, or simply "not deep," but here's what has become self-evident to me: *We start living with desperation when we get honest about how desperate we really are.* In other words, when we begin to own the depth of our pain, emptiness, and loneliness—and the inability of other lovers to meet the needs of our hearts—we'll find ourselves desperately longing for Jesus in a way that moves us to seek him and his love, moment by moment, like never before. This is exactly what John of the Cross declares in his *Dark Night of the Soul*, a mystical treatise birthed in 1577 during nine months in a Spanish prison. John says the darkness is where "the yearnings for God become so great . . . that [our] very bones seem to be dried up by [our] thirst" for him—and a deep longing for "Divine love begins to be enkindled in [our] spirit."[7] In other words, it's in the darkness—whether the natural darkness of living in a fallen world or a specific, personalized darkness allowed by God's severe mercy—that our desperation for him is born, *a desperation we must allow ourselves to consistently feel if we want to consistently abide.*

My friend Clarence was raised in an abusive home, got out as soon as he could, and by age twenty was an apprentice ironworker. He shared with me recently, "Today it's different, but when I first started, if you didn't do what all the guys were doing, they didn't want you around." That meant drinking and drugging—even on the job.

"I was high every day up on the iron, sometimes hundreds of feet in the air," Clarence said. "Every time my foot slipped, what came out of my mouth was 'O, God.' But when I didn't fall, I'd go back to thinking, *God is for old people.* I can't believe I survived." Clarence worked iron for thirty years and loved it. "We got a lot of respect from the other trades," he remembered. "Their respect kept me from thinking about how I didn't respect myself. They made me feel bigger than I was."

Along the way, Clarence became a heroin addict. But he also met and married Alberta, who introduced him to the love of Jesus. He started going to church, went to treatment a few times—but never stopped using for very long. "I was convinced I could do life my way," Clarence told me.

By the time Clarence and I met, God was mercifully allowing Clarence's life to fall apart. "After I retired," he said, "it got so bad that five minutes after Alberta left for work in the morning, I'd be off to buy dope. I got scared I was going to die because I knew how many times I should have died already—falling drunk off the iron, an overdose, or getting beat in the dope house. And . . . I was petrified I was going to lose my family. I hadn't just come to the end of the road; I'd hit a wall that had fallen on top of me."

Finally, like the Prodigal Son, Clarence "came to his senses" (Luke 15:17, NLT). After a long pause, he whispered, "I had no other place to go . . . but Jesus." Desperate, Clarence entered a Christian treatment center, got clean, and lived clean for two years. And then he relapsed. Remember, desperation isn't a one-time fix but a lifetime way of being with Jesus. "I was so embarrassed and afraid of how people would look at me," Clarence remembered, "but I went back to the same treatment facility anyway." It was there, during his seventh time in rehab, that two miracles occured. First, when he was in detox, a staff lady spoke directly and powerfully to his shame. "Don't forget, my brother," she said passionately, "Jesus forgives us seventy times seven." Clarence wept. It was a turning point. And then, for the seventh time, Alberta said, "I love you, Clarence. God loves you. Get well." Miraculously, this time around . . . her words landed.

That was five years ago. Today, Clarence is a well-loved and respected husband, father, grandfather, and brother. He leads both a men's and a Narcotics Anonymous group at our church. And his relationship with God? Last night, I called Clarence and asked. The phone got quiet—and then he said, "The truth is, I just can't live without him." Indeed.

And then . . . there's me. On that life-changing night in 1990, I ran with abandon from a dark religion of rules and a lying lover named Performance—toward a Jesus who compassionately embraced *me* and smothered *me* with the kisses of the Father. Today I abide in

Jesus Christ, not because I'm painstakingly spiritual, but because I'm desperately, madly in love.

But let me be clear, lest you misunderstand and picture me walking around in some spiritually utopian state, living beyond life's pain because of my passion for him. Nothing could be further from the truth. For me, desperation is birthed from gritty, unflinching honesty in the midst of daily pain that cannot be ignored. Two days ago, my eighty-seven-year-old father was admitted to the hospital with COVID-19, and I'm 250 miles away with no way to get to him—or my mother—because of strict visiting protocols and my own health issues. Our girls and their families are thirteen hundred miles away, and we haven't seen them in five months—the longest stretch apart in over thirty-five years. Life is painful and hard, and I so often feel alone, empty, spiritually exhausted—and desperate for intimacy with my God through his Son, Jesus Christ. Today, my heart is fixated passionately on him . . . because nothing else will do.

Frederick Buechner says, "Love is not merely a warmth to bask in . . . but a grave, fierce yearning and reaching out for Paradise itself."[8] Do you feel that yearning? Are you done—really done—with whatever, whoever you've been desperately pursuing? Are you tired of the spiritual exhaustion . . . the frustration, confusion, and discouragement, the years of unsustainable "do more, try harder" Christianity? Then, like King David, Peter and Paul, Augustine of Hippo and Catherine of Siena, like Clarence, Sophia, me and Leigh Anne, and so many other sons and daughters of God in history—let your desperation bring you to your knees. Let your longing compel you to cry out, right now, to Jesus of Nazareth, your One Great Love. He is with you. He will hear you. He will embrace you. And together, you will step into the abiding life.

Chapter 3

LONGING FOR HEALING

He has sent Me to heal the brokenhearted.

LUKE 4:18

*My soul is being healed. I'm bathing in Him. When He comes,
He removes the hurt, the bitterness, the soreness. He removes
the tiredness. . . . He comforts the soul. Thank You, Jesus.
He's here. Thank God for the Lamb.*

THOMASINA NEELY

Abiding in Jesus' love means learning to see Jesus as our Healer.

"I just got a text from Chrissy." Sue looked up at me with panicky eyes. It was Sunday morning at Hope Community Church, and she was sitting in the second row. "She's at a drug house, she's using again, and she wants a ride—to anywhere. What do I do?"

Heroin had landed Chrissy in prison a few years earlier. Sue, twenty-five years clean from heroin herself, had been walking alongside her through letters. When Chrissy was released, she quickly joined us at Hope, committed to learning to live free. For a while, Chrissy had done exactly that. She was a regular in Sunday worship and had begun the healing work of unpacking deeper layers of her backstory—including serious soul wounds and the ways, over the years, she had tried to mask the pain. Now, suddenly, she was back on the street, dying . . . but still she was reaching out for the unconditional love her heart was longing for.

I immediately stopped what we were doing in worship and looked intently at the small crowd of Jesus followers in front of me. "One of our sisters is hurting and acting out of her pain," I said. "We need to ask God what his love would call us to do." Almost immediately, Dave, sitting close by, tapped Sue on the shoulder.

"We need to go get her," he said. "Now." Dave, along with his wife, Sarah, had involved Chrissy in their young family and had even given her a job in Dave's business. So, without saying another word to me or the others, Dave and Sue rushed out the back door of the building while the rest of us did the best we could to continue with the service.

An hour later, I had just finished praying over the bread and cup of Communion when I looked up to see a holy threesome slowly, deliberately shuffling down the aisle toward the crucified Jesus. Chrissy was in the middle—eyes glazed, head drooping, legs wobbling, arms clinging to the necks of wounded healers Dave and Sue as they literally carried her broken body and spirit to the cross and helped her eat and drink the life-giving body and blood of Christ. As I watched, I wept. First, for Chrissy—but also, I think, for all of us. Because in Chrissy's sinfulness and brokenness, we saw our own. In Chrissy's Sunday-morning pilgrimage from the drug house to the cross, we saw who *we* are and what we're really looking for. Like Chrissy, we're not only rebellious but also critically wounded. Like Chrissy, we not only need forgiveness . . . but healing. Healing that Jesus himself said he came to bring our sinful, broken world.

Consider the mysterious-yet-breathtaking scene it must have been: A thirty-year-old young man stands in his hometown Nazareth synagogue, invited by the elders to conduct the traditional Sabbath reading from one of the prophets. "I think it's Joseph's son, Jesus, recently come home," a few seasoned worshipers whisper back and forth—but for the most part, the crowd is strangely quiet, as if anticipating something unusual, even noteworthy about to happen. The ruler of the synagogue carefully places the Isaiah scroll in Jesus' hands, and Jesus very deliberately rolls out the sacred manuscript almost to the end—to Isaiah's hope-filled prophecy about a Deliverer who would come in the name of Israel's God, finally enacting her promised, longed-for rescue.

"The Spirit of the LORD is upon Me, because He has anointed Me to preach the gospel to the poor . . . to *heal* the brokenhearted, to proclaim *liberty* to the captives,"[1] Jesus reads, and the prophet's words descend like balm on hearts deeply wounded and despairing after centuries of oppression and seeming abandonment. Spellbound, the small synagogue crowd gazes at Jesus with anxious anticipation as he hands the scroll back to the attendant and calmly takes his seat, readying himself to offer expected commentary. Seconds pass like days. Finally Jesus utters these history-altering words: "Today this Scripture is fulfilled in your hearing" (Luke 4:16-21). Or, put more simply: "I'm the One."

In that profound, historic hour, Jesus publicly claimed and proclaimed his messianic mission, not only to Israel but to the world. He took on the prophetic mantle of rescuing God's sons and daughters from the devastating impact of centuries of sin—our own sin as well as the pain we experience from the sins of others. He owned Isaiah's image of "the Healer," the One whose powerful ministry of binding up humanity's brokenness would somehow unbolt sin's dungeon and begin to set us free. That first-century Sabbath in Nazareth's synagogue, Jesus not only implied that one day he would heal the entire cosmos but promised that he would be your healer and mine—today. Now. In real time. A promise intended to surround and empower a lifetime of abiding in Jesus' love.

The problem is, I'm not sure most of us believe him. Eternal healing, yes. And, as well, much of the church has historically believed that God heals physically, though amid much disagreement about who, how, and how often. But do we believe that Jesus came to heal what's usually left out in much of modern Christianity—our souls, our psyches, our lives in this very moment, as we wrestle with the powers of darkness? Do we believe Jesus heals *damaged emotions*? Emotions like shame, despair, rage, fear, jealousy, and pride, or a myriad of *debilitating false beliefs* like *I'm stupid* or *There's no forgiveness for what I've done* or *I don't need anyone* or *If people knew me, they would reject me*. Do we believe that Jesus' promise of healing includes the satanically induced *trauma* we've all experienced—in childhood or marriage, or through relational betrayal, catastrophic illness, or natural disaster? Or have we bought the insidious lie that in our struggle with hell in these areas commonly termed *psychological*—where wounds devastate our hearts, influence our behavior patterns, and damage our ability to hear and obey God's voice—Jesus is more like our spiritual-life coach, cheering us on and reminding us of Bible verses we need to obey as we grind out our spiritual journey . . . on our own?[2]

I'm convinced many of us have so completely lost touch with Isaiah's promise of a healing Messiah, we've persuaded ourselves that other than when we're physically ill, we don't really need healing. That what we long for in our war against sin is to be more disciplined, more committed, or more knowledgeable. That what we really need is to stop whining about our pain, join two more Bible studies, see the spiritual task ahead . . . and "just do it." No wonder it's so difficult for us to envision Christianity as a lifetime of abiding in Jesus' love—a love intended not to simply move us to know more and try harder but to heal our brokenness and set us free.

I remember well the evening in 1979, two years into our marriage and shortly before Carla's graduation from Taylor University, when she and I met with an older, mentor-like pastor and his wife. I had dropped out of Dallas Theological Seminary after my first year—yes, to get married, but primarily because I didn't think I fit the "holiness" standard for being a pastor. But in the next two and a half years, as Carla finished her degree and I worked a couple of different jobs to support us, I got that "deep in the gut" sense that maybe this shepherding thing was built into my spiritual DNA. So, as we prepared to go back to seminary, we not only had questions that called for wisdom but felt anxiety that craved emotional support. Carla was less than excited about the ridiculous expectations facing a pastor's spouse, and I was still worried I wasn't Christian enough.

I honestly can't recall what counsel this very caring couple gave my wife. But I vividly remember my interaction with this brother pastor, mostly because of our conversation's bizarre conclusion. I opened our dialogue with, "I'm serious about Jesus, I love people deeply, and in the last few years, my pastoral gifts have been affirmed over and over." After a self-conscious pause, I continued, "But the truth is, I still wrestle with intense anger that's plagued me since I was a kid." He listened thoughtfully while I shared a few more anger details—and then he asked his first "just do it" question. Had I memorized all the anger passages in the Bible?

"Are you kidding me?" I replied. "I've studied them so many times I've memorized them all without even trying."

He went on to further probe my spiritual journey about other disciplines like prayer, and I think he eventually asked if I had an accountability partner. His questions were almost all about how hard I'd worked to overcome sin and walk with God, and my answers were dutifully perfect and true—because, leading up to that evening, "just do it" Christianity had been the core reality of my spiritual life.

Remember, I was the church kid who played by the rules, always doing the right thing, readily confessing sin after failure, and always trying harder to do better the next time. I was devout and disciplined, consistently studying the Bible, serious about understanding what God was teaching me. I preached my first sermon at age fourteen and over the years led almost every youth group, prayer group, or Bible study I was involved with—including, at the time of that conversation, a neighborhood Bible study in the mobile-home community where we lived as a young married couple. I was so fanatical about "obedience" that early in our marriage I sadly remember consistently criticizing Carla's relationship with Jesus—including the time I told her she should trash her stack of *People* magazines to free up space for Bible study, to which she quickly and appropriately retorted, "Mind your own business."

So of course I had the right answers to the pastor's questions about my anger. The problem was, the "study harder, grit your teeth more fiercely" pathway to spirituality had failed me. No amount of effort, guilt, consequences, rebuke, or middle-of-the-night promises had helped me overcome my crippling anger. I could listen to well-delivered, lofty sermons on "the power of the Resurrection" or "the sanctifying ministry of the Holy Spirit," but they did little to curb my abrasive tongue, stop me from pounding my fist on a countertop, or prevent me from occasionally punching a hole in our thin mobile-home walls. I remember one day almost losing my job as a supervisor in a sheltered workshop because I was so angry with my boss that I slammed my fist through the drywall in the break room. Even the self-discipline that had served me so well as a scholar athlete in both high school and college—driving me to study longer and work out harder than most—was no match for my rage.

Listen carefully: What I know now but didn't know then is that in God's economy, sermons, Scripture, discipline, trying harder, and even prayer, by themselves, were never meant to mitigate the pain of damaged emotions. My out-of-control anger needed the healing of Jesus Christ.

So do we all. A few years back, Jerome approached me in my car one frozen Detroit day, asking for help. I invited him into the front seat of my toasty warm, dark-green 1999 Dodge Durango, and he poured out his story. He was fifteen. He'd never known his father, and his mother had wrestled for years with a heroin addiction. A school dropout who often crashed on the couches of different associates in our struggling neighborhood and ate when he could—Jerome was desperate for a Wendy's Baconator that icy day . . . and even more desperate for some hope. He asked if I could help him. I said I would try, and for the next several years, we walked together.

It was a rocky relationship, mostly because Jerome, though somewhat motivated to grow, was also a deeply wounded young man. He was in and out of trouble—I still have a note he wrote me from the Wayne County jail, complete with his personal take on one of David's hope-filled psalms. I remember how one day, Jerome and I sat in my office, talking about the importance of knowing we are loved. He said to me—in a rare moment of tender candor—"Pastor Kevin, let me tell you something. If my mother just took time to tell me when to be home at night, I would know she loved me. But she never has—because she doesn't." And the tears ran down the face of this tough-as-nails kid from the streets of Detroit. It was the only time I ever saw him cry.

Eventually, Jerome believed in Jesus, and one Easter morning, I was honored to baptize him. A Kingdom-of-God victory for sure—and lots of Luke 15 partying and gratitude! But the very next day, I drove up to the church building on the corner of Jefferson and Marlborough, glanced down the street to my left, and saw folks rushing out their front doors to their porches. There was Jerome, shirtless and angry, stomping with long, intense strides down that same street toward a brawl about to go down. I jumped out of the Durango, sprinted to his side, wrapped my arm around his waist, and with adrenaline-aided passion and love, hauled him away from the impending disaster. Through gritted teeth, I whispered, "What the heck, son? I just baptized you yesterday!"

But here's the point: What did I expect from a young believer who had experienced so much *trauma* (years-worth of life-eviscerating experiences), who was filled with deeply imbedded *false beliefs* (such as *I'm not loved, I'll never have enough, I'll never be enough,* and *Only violence wins*), and whose heart was overflowing with *damaged emotions* (shame, rage, depression, hopelessness) that tormented and overwhelmed his spirit every day? Did I really think a few dozen Sunday sermons and Wednesday-afternoon pizza-infused Bible studies, combined with stern words of pastoral warning and rebuke, would somehow magically transform this broken young man into a smiling, Christianized obedience machine? Jerome needed the Word of God, and like all of us, he had choices that only he could make about his life. But Jesus didn't call Jerome to obedience in a vacuum. He called him to a faithfulness that is the fruit of abiding in God's healing, freeing love.

Let me say it again: This healing isn't just for wannabe pastors with anger issues or young men from a broken family and neighborhood. It's for all of us. Each of us must come to the same conclusion

I was coming to years ago sitting in my pastor friend's living room—and that young Jerome, now in his late twenties, is still inching his way toward: that no amount of trying harder, Bible memory, or well-intentioned prayers of resolve will heal the damage that creates chaos in our lives. We must turn toward the Luke 4 Jesus that came to set the captives free—the Jesus that calls us to live life abiding in his love. It's a crucial crossroad each of us *must* face and a conclusion each of us *must* reach if we're going to embrace the abiding life. Because the life-coach Jesus of "just do it" Christianity is not the compassionate, healing Jesus who invites us to surrender to his powerful love.

On that late-1970s evening of counseling, I was moving quickly toward that crucial crossroad. When there were finally no more questions, I remember the four of us sitting in uncomfortable silence while my pastor friend contemplated what to say or do next. Eventually, with compassionate regret, he shared his verdict: "Here's the deal, Kev. If you can't overcome your own sin, how can you help others overcome theirs? I'm sorry, but I guess you'll need to find a different career—because the truth is, if you can't deal with your anger, being a pastor isn't for you." I was stunned. I thought, *Wait, that's it? Jesus forgives me for my past, promises me an eternal future—but all he offers me in my sin and pain today is a Christianized version of spiritual behavior modification? And if that doesn't work, oh well?* I was devastated. I knew there had to be more. But even after years of studying the Bible and going to church, at that moment, I didn't know what *more* was.

After an awkward closing prayer, Carla and I left—and ended up in seminary anyway. We eventually graduated, had our first baby girl, landed in our first church, and then after our second sweetheart was born three years later, we moved to a second parish in Detroit. But here's the bottom line: In the eleven years following that night of "pastoral counsel," I studied, preached, loved, and performed my heart out—all the while battling my baggage, especially my anger, the best I knew how. But it wasn't until after the severe mercy of that dark night on a Detroit freeway that I began to understand.

Our hearts aren't only deeply sinful . . . they're also profoundly wounded beyond human repair. Our minds, spirits, emotions, and wills have been traumatized by an enemy who steals, kills and destroys (John 10:10). What we need is so much more than a benevolent deity who calls us to a life-giving path, because as hard as we try, we can't stay on it. What our hearts long for is One who sees our bondage to wound and sin, feels our pain, and loves us so much that he is willing to sacrifice all to come to us, heal us, and set us free.

In my brokenness and despair—the rotten fruit of a "just do it" Christian life—I began to look at the Jesus of the Gospels and really see him for the very first time. He wasn't glaring at me with disappointment or sternly pointing to the next spiritual task. Instead, he looked at me with serious but compassionate eyes, and I began to hear him say, "I love you, Kev. And I see you—your sin, your wounds, and your pain. I've come to heal you, my brother, and to free you to be all the Father created you to be. So unclench your fists, get your eyes off the rules . . . and come walk with me." Today, I realize he was simply saying, "Abide in my love."

I'm praying—hard—that some of you feel hopeful that Jesus really did come to heal you and you can finally let go of the exhausting foolishness of trying to save yourself from the power and damage of sin. But some of you also might be a little confused. I get it. Because these two opposite and contradictory ways of viewing our life with God have been at war with one another for a long, long time. In fact, in his profound work *Repenting of Religion*, Greg Boyd suggests the battle began at the very beginning, in the Garden of Eden. God created Adam and Eve out of love, and they lived with him in perfect, intimate community—every need and longing fulfilled by the love they shared. Enter the serpent muttering, "It's not enough," lying to God's first son and daughter, tricking them into believing that there was another "something" in the Garden that God wanted to keep for himself, a valuable "something" that would give them a life God's love alone could never offer. That "something" was the knowledge of good and evil, a knowledge God had lovingly protected them from, not only because he knew they weren't created to handle it but also because he knew what that knowledge would lead to: obsession with and mishandling of a rules-oriented, effort-based relationship with him that would ultimately destroy them.[3]

You know the rest of the story. Adam and Eve chose knowledge of good and evil over love—and in that moment, "just do it" religion was born. Until then, obedience had always been synonymous with God's love and flowed from Adam and Eve's trusting, intimate relationship with him. But immediately after believing the enemy's lie that God's love wasn't enough, they began trying to "get life" from their understanding and control of good and evil[4]—the rules—and obeying God instantly became an impossible-to-discern, insecure, self-centered, judgmental, death-dealing chore. As Bonhoeffer notes, "Man now lives only out of his own self, out of his knowledge of good and evil, and in this he is dead."[5] One Genesis chapter later, Adam and Eve's son Abel *was* dead.

These two very antithetical ways of looking at our relationship with God have been fiercely debated since. In late antiquity, it was Pelagius's "will and effort" sparring with Augustine's "we stand in need of God's grace."[6] In the Middle Ages, it was the vast, meticulous theological knowledge of Thomas Aquinas contrasted with the passion of mystics like Catherine of Siena or monks like Bernard of

Clairvaux—theologically brilliant but known for the priority they placed on intimacy with the God they loved.

Then came the Reformation and its renewed emphasis on preaching, which was contemporaneous with the invention of the printing press, making the content of the Bible readily available to believers for the first time in church history. These events, coupled with the ensuing Enlightenment and its focus on human reason, ensured that for the last few hundred years, Christianity has been more than ever about our ability to know good and evil—and our effort to obey what we think we know. Today, many of us offer a humble shout-out to the power of our love relationship with God, when what we really believe is that if we're studious and disciplined enough, we can master our own spiritual fate. And just like in the Garden, the serpent has us by the throat . . . again.

Let me be perfectly clear: I love the Bible. I believe it is God-breathed, authoritative, and profoundly necessary for our spiritual battle with the powers of darkness. The margins of my own copy of the Scripture that I've used in my life with God for the last twenty-five years are so full of personal notes, theological thoughts and questions, Greek and Hebrew words, and one-line personal prayers, there's almost no white space left.

What I don't believe, however, is that Scripture was ever meant to stand alone—or even alongside our sincere efforts to obey—to deliver us from the brokenness of sin. The Bible isn't a book of spiritual incantations to be recited in a war of words with hell and its minions. The Word's power to help us overcome sin has always been intimately connected to and dependent on our love relationship with the God of the Word—and since the coming of Jesus, specifically dependent on abiding in *his* love. Remember his words to the Pharisees: "You have your heads in your Bibles constantly because you think you'll find eternal life there. But you miss the forest for the trees. These Scriptures are all about *me*! And here I am, standing right before you, and you aren't willing to receive from me the life you say you want" (John 5:39-40, MSG). As N. T. Wright comments, "Christian teachers can talk till they're blue in the face, but unless their hearers have . . . this awareness of the true God loving them and shaping their lives in a new way, it won't produce genuine disciples."[7]

Is it any wonder then, that bleeding-out Israel flocked to Jesus of Nazareth when he rejected the knowledge-of-good-and-evil, rules-based, human-effort-ridden philosophy of the Pharisees—and instead embodied the all-sufficient love of the God of Eden? Jesus was calling sinful, wounded Israel to come back home to an intimacy with God that had always been the only sustainable source of obedience, back to the healing they needed for their sin-damaged lives. And so, Jesus healed—not only broken, diseased bodies but also broken, diseased psyches, hearts, and spirits. He forgave freely, signaling that the cosmic wound of sin is at the root of all human pain and that forgiveness is a spiritual, yet also emotional healing we all desperately need. He delivered many who were tormented by demons and more than once thrust his healing hand into the realm of the dead, gripping children of God with his relentless love and bringing them back to life. In three powerful years of compassionate ministry to Israel's wounded, Jesus of Nazareth consistently stared down the powers of darkness, making it clear that, since the day he arrived on the scene as Yahweh's healer, they were hopelessly overmatched.

Alfred Edersheim concludes that Jesus of Nazareth's comprehensive healing ministry in the Gospels proves that God's intent has *always* been to deliver *all* his broken sons and daughters "from *all* the woe which sin had brought."[8] And though this "restor[ation] [to] fulness and completeness" will only be absolute in the coming

Kingdom, Jesus came to deliver a healing deposit on that future *now*.[9] Healing that includes not only the marginalized-and-abused woman at the well; lost Zacchaeus; shame-based, emotionally broken Peter; and countless others in first-century Israel—but also beloved, wounded sons and daughters of God like you and me.

So, how does all this connect with Jesus' strong call to "abide in My love"? First, because when he looks at us, his love sees our brokenness and moves toward us with compassion (Matthew 9:36). When the rich young ruler approached Jesus with spiritual and emotional anguish about eternal life, Mark says, "Jesus, looking at him, loved him" (Mark 10:21). When the desperate leper threw himself down at Jesus' feet, Jesus didn't just heal him but was "moved with compassion" by his pain (Mark 1:41). Believe it or not, that's exactly how Jesus feels about *us* in our wounded and even sometimes rebellious state. He literally can't stand to see us hurt, so his compassionate love constantly reaches out to us, inviting us to come close—to abide in him. His love won't have it any other way.

But there's more. Jesus' love doesn't just move him to care for us in our pain—*his love is the power that heals our pain*. Jesus heals us because he loves us, and it's his love that heals us—a love that crushed the death-dealing powers of darkness at the Cross. No wonder that when Matthew comments on Jesus' power to heal, he looks back at the Cross, where Jesus' love triumphed over evil, and declares, "He Himself took our infirmities and bore our sicknesses" (Matthew 8:17).[10] No wonder Peter calls the persecuted church in Asia Minor to entrust their struggling, wounded selves to him who "bore our sins in His own body on the tree . . . by whose stripes you were healed" (1 Peter 2:24). No wonder Jesus himself adamantly calls us to abide in his love because only there—*nowhere else*—can we find victory over sin and healing from its pain.

While I was writing this book, a gifted Christian author—who some years ago penned a bestseller offering a "just do it," fail-safe pathway of rules and discipline—publicly confessed that what he had written to thousands . . . hadn't worked for him. The last I read, he's wrestling with whether to continue following Jesus at all. I hurt for this brother because I've felt the confusion and despair he's experiencing.

The truth is, *nowhere else* means nowhere else. Anyone staying on a "just do it" pathway for long . . . always ends up at the same despairing destination.

First, we *lie*, pretending all is well in our walk with God because we're too ashamed to confess our struggle. Then, eventually, we begin to *hide*, either by avoiding those who ask us real questions about the state of our heart and life or by masking our brokenness behind our obedience to a carefully selected list of spiritual rules that artificially make us feel like all is well. Finally—and this may take years—we simply *quit*. We may not walk away completely or come close to suicide, like I did. We might "quit" more subtly, quietly showing up for church every week with a forced Christian smile, engaging in clichéd, Christianese conversation, and maybe even serving in a ministry. But inside, we're dead, resigned to living with damaged emotions, raging false beliefs, unhealed trauma, and the resulting sinful behavior patterns and broken relationships—combined with feeling distant from a God we've never been able to please. All while the world around us rots because we have nothing of substance to offer their pain. And our healing Jesus stands off to the side, looking on . . . with tears.

Remember the crossroad I referred to earlier? We've arrived. And if we're serious about abiding in Jesus' love, here's where we face a crucial question each of us must answer for ourselves: *Who is the real*

Jesus of Nazareth? Is he Isaiah's healing Messiah, beckoning us to a lifelong, intimate relationship of surrender to his love, compelling us to focus on him, love him, and trust him to do for us what we cannot do for ourselves? Or is he the Lord of "just do it" Christianity, relentlessly commanding us to know more and try harder, directing us to the power of self in our battle against sin? Because the truth is, he cannot be both. One is the Son of God. The other, an imposter. One heals us and sets us free. The other leads us to our death. If we follow one, we will not and cannot follow the other.

The bottom line is this: *When we see Jesus as our Healer, then and only then will we choose to abide in his powerful love*—and begin to experience victory over sin and the wounds it causes.

It's been almost thirty years since that dark night when "just do it" Jesus almost killed me—and the real Jesus of Nazareth saved me and began to heal my shame-based, rage-filled, broken heart. I'll share much more about the healing process in the pages ahead, but this I can tell you now: There's no explanation for who I am as a man today, except for his healing love.

Let me be clear: I still wrestle daily with the powers of darkness. But Jesus Christ and his powerful love are healing me still. I struggle with working too much, but I no longer work to be loved. I still sometimes battle with anger, but I don't live angry. I fight shame, but it no longer controls me. Like anyone else, I occasionally struggle in relationships, but more often than not, I love Carla, my family, and all kinds of people so intensely that it's hard for me to be at a restaurant or a baseball game without getting tears in my eyes, wondering, *Do they know?*—longing to sit with each one, showing them how much they're valued by the God who values me. I still grapple with a deep-seated fear that life might ask me to bury one of my daughters, wondering if my faith could survive. And sometimes the pervasive, unrelenting pain I see in the world around me causes me—for a moment—to doubt God's existence. But so far, even here, in my trembling, his love runs deeper still.

Maybe most importantly, after years of obsessing about Christian rules and how to obey them, today I really don't think about them much at all. My walk with Jesus isn't about a list of anything. It's about him and his love. Just today, after a long four months of traveling, speaking, and counseling, I felt depressed and alone, wondering aloud how I could write a book about abiding in Jesus' love when all I could see was darkness. Carla tenderly reminded me, "You're human and you're tired. Your feelings are overwhelming you today—but Jesus is still here. He's with you. He loves you. You're looking to him in your weariness and pain. And that's what it means to abide." Indeed.

What if this day you could sit very near the Jesus of Luke 4, feel his compassionate arm around your weary shoulders, and hear him gently say, "Dearest sister, don't be afraid. My brother, you don't need to run or hide ever again—because I love you. Stop obsessing about the rules and let go of trying to manufacture the strength to obey them. I see your desire to follow me, but I also see your weakness and wounds and feel your unhealed pain. Here's my promise: I'm not going to shame you or coerce you into obedience. If you'll let me, if you'll trust me, if you'll simply walk with me, making your home in my love, I will slowly, surely heal you . . . and set you free."

Several weeks ago, I met with a young brother who came to this same crossroad some years earlier. An ex-athlete himself who, like me, was coached to believe that strength and discipline are everything, my friend had to learn that there were areas of his life and his relationship with Jesus Christ that strength and discipline couldn't touch. One day, in a moment of deeply transformative clarity, he penned this four-line hymn of surrender to God's answer to his brokenness:

I am a sinner, and I need saving.
I have wounds, and I need healing.
I have suffered, and I need relief.
My soul has experienced destruction, and I need life.[11]

Is your broken, struggling heart ready to whisper this prayer to Jesus, the God-man from Nazareth, who loves you so much he took all your sin and pain on himself at the Cross? It's time to heal. It's time to start abiding in his love.

Chapter 4

SURRENDER

*I appeal to you therefore, brothers and sisters, by the mercies of God,
to present your bodies as a living sacrifice, holy and acceptable to God,
which is your spiritual worship.*

ROMANS 12:1, NRSV

*God does everything . . . only because the soul has totally surrendered
herself to him. And this surrender is the highest act of her freedom.*

EDITH STEIN (SAINT TERESA BENEDICTA OF THE CROSS)

Abiding in Jesus' love is learning to live surrendered to him.

IT MIGHT SOUND like a strange thing to say after a chapter on healing, but right now, I'm a wreck. Two days ago, a beautiful, brilliant,
strong, Christ-loving young man in our Hope Community took his
own life. I know he's in glory—the Cross and empty tomb make
it so. But I'm still standing toe to toe with Jesus, pounding on his
chest, begging him to tell me what I could have done—and why
he didn't do more—to save the precious life of this son of God. I'm
imploring him to whisper to a brokenhearted mom that he's got her
baby boy and he's got her and she's going to get through this. And
while I have his attention, I'm pleading with him to heal a brother
whose cancer has returned, to touch a marriage in danger, to mend

racial wounds in a church I love very much, to give hope to a young pastor getting pummeled by misguided leaders, to come with power and mercy to the family of a young woman recently shot—and to forgive me for the dismissive way I spoke to Carla just this morning, from a heart nearly overcome by the smoke and blood of spiritual battle all around.

Why am I telling you all of this? Maybe first to remind you that what I'm sharing about walking with Jesus is true not only when blessings are flowing but also when Jesus' followers are taking on enemy fire—pain, fear, and despair abounding. And second, in a book about "how" to abide in Jesus' love, you might be expecting, by now, a little more specific guidance on "abiding" practices like prayer, confession of sin, reading the Bible, and telling others about Jesus. But the truth is, *in life-threatening battle scenarios we face in this life, spiritual practices only have power to the extent that they emerge from a deeply internalized love relationship with Jesus.* When his love becomes *everything* to us, when we get *desperate* for his love, when we begin to see our need for healing and Jesus as our only *Healer*—only then will we devour the truth of Scripture in a way that heals and transforms. Only then will we run to him authentically in prayer with every need, fear, hope, and dream. Only then will we boldly brag about him to others with the passion of a teenager newly in love. So, yes, we must eventually talk about the disciplines and practices that nourish our intimacy with Jesus, but without being "rooted and grounded" in his love (Ephesians 3:17-19), our spiritual practices will be hollow, temporary, and powerless.

Which brings me to the next deep-seated layer of "how" we abide—and along with it, one of the most terrifying, faith-challenging experiences of my life.[1] It was February 7, 2017. Carla and I had just traveled across Michigan from our metro-Detroit home to a suburban-Chicago hospital to see our newest grandson, Van, born the day before. We were in the gift shop, looking for flowers for my daughter Andrea and something Chicago Cubs for little Van, when Carla received a phone call from her endocrinologist. It wasn't an unexpected call—we had been waiting on biopsy results for a growth on Carla's thyroid—but the news we received was both startling and devastating.

"You need to find a place to be alone," Carla's doctor gently told us. We walked around the corner to a small, empty conference room. My best friend of forty years and I huddled around her phone, holding onto each other, begging Jesus to hold onto us. "I'm sorry to tell you this, Carla," the doctor compassionately continued, "but you have cancer."

She went on to explain that the specific kind of cancer invading Carla's thyroid was not the type usually easily and effectively treated but a kind statistically more rare, invasive, and destructive. Months later, after more testing, we found out that, in fact, the type of cancer Carla had was so rare, there were fewer than one hundred documented cases in the world. All we knew at the time was that the doctor seemed very concerned for Carla's future—and we were afraid. So, after bowing our heads and tearfully mumbling a cry of help to God, we elevatored our way to Andrea, her husband, Dusty, and their new little boy. What joy to embrace our kids and to watch Carla reach out and receive little Van into her grandmother arms for the first time! Then, as you might expect, she broke down sobbing, reluctantly pouring out her frightening news. And our journey into the cancerous valley of the shadow of death began.

I wish I could tell you that in the days and months following—as we walked the well-worn pathway of appointments and blood tests, treatment options and surgery consults—I went to a deep place with God, trusting him more than ever. But the truth is, one day I realized that for the most part, I'd stopped talking to God at all. I wanted one thing from him: to let me know that my Carla would beat cancer. To tell me that his beloved daughter—the most gifted teacher and profound lover of children I had ever known; a woman who saw the magnificent beauty of God in every bird, flower, and sunset and whose laughter and creativity brought healing to our broken world; and most importantly, my best friend, who had loved me for a lifetime more completely than I'd ever been loved—would live. Of course, I knew theologically that rain falls "on the just and on the unjust" (Matthew 5:45) and that the God who gave no answers or assurances to Job wasn't likely to be any different with me. I didn't care. As I stared into the fearful abyss of possibly living without this woman who was my soul—until I heard "she's going to be fine," I basically told God, "talk to my hand."

Buechner says, "The trouble with steeling yourself against the harshness of reality is that the same steel that secures your life against being destroyed secures your life also against being opened up and transformed by the holy power that life itself comes from."[2] When we are afraid—and I was petrified—we naturally want to control our circumstances and destiny. But control is an archenemy of the abiding life because whatever or whoever we grip, we block from the protective, life-giving, powerful love of Jesus. By holding Carla's life, her destiny, and our relationship so firmly in my hands, I kept at bay the securing love of Jesus my heart longed for. And as for Carla, instead of experiencing the presence of Jesus through me as her best friend, she at first mostly felt the emotional death grip of my well-intentioned control.

Several weeks into living out my fearful, stubborn boundary with God, I was reading a book by author Bekah DiFelice—and suddenly, the God I told to leave me alone showed up anyway. DiFelice spoke about her Marine husband, Mike, deploying to an area in Afghanistan where casualties were common—and how afraid she was that he might never come home. Taking Jesus' words to his disciples on prayer to heart (Luke 11:9), she found herself "knocking and banging" on God's door, "begging for assurances" that her husband would "come home alive and with all of his limbs."[3] Given where I was presently with my fear of losing Carla, my heart inhaled every word.

But what DiFelice said next was straight from God's mouth. Somewhere along the way, in her battle with God for her husband's life, she had "misunderstood prayer as a way to control God rather than a pathway of surrender to him."[4]

Control . . . or surrender. The atmosphere around me became instantly still. And for the first time in forever, I looked into the loving eyes of a God who clearly knew my heart, who understood my dread over the possibility of losing Carla, who didn't shame me for my anxiety-ridden demands and stubborn relational holdout. Instead, he pursued me like a Father missing his son. His compassionate gaze compelled me to come home.

With tears, I got up from the chair where I had been reading and began pacing back and forth over our thick black-and-tan rug, pouring out several weeks of blood tests and oncology appointments and fears to my Abba. More importantly, for the first time in weeks, I listened. Though he didn't speak in audible words, this is what I heard God say in an unmistakably clear way:

> Listen to me, son. Carla isn't yours—she's mine. You cannot love her well by gripping her tightly. To love her, you must surrender her to me. I'm not promising the outcome of Carla's battle with cancer. You don't get to know the future. What I promise is that I love you, and I will be with you and Carla, and I will never leave you. Ever.

In that moment—I let go. I turned my dearest friend and deepest earthly love over to the One who loves her most. I surrendered Carla— her body, her spirit, her cancer, her future, her life—to the One who gave her life to begin with. And—please don't miss this—in that moment of surrender, I began to abide in the love of my Jesus and experience love's power, peace, and freedom that refuses to coexist with control.

Buechner says that "the one thing a clenched fist cannot do is accept, even from [God] himself, a helping hand"[5]—even if that hand contains powerful, unconditional love. So, to abide in the love of Jesus, we must unclench our fists, letting go of whoever or whatever we're holding onto with a controlling grip—and surrender, all of it, to Jesus and his love.

Surrender is the first and most important discipline of our abiding life with Jesus. It's a discipline because we must choose. We won't surrender to him until we're convinced his love is everything, until we're desperate for his love, until we see him as our loving, compassionate Healer, longing to set us free. To state it precisely: We can't abide in Jesus if we don't surrender—and we won't surrender if we don't know and trust his love.

Paul says exactly that to Jesus followers in ancient Rome, in what might be the most striking "surrender" text in the entire New Testament:

> I appeal to you therefore, brothers and sisters, by the mercies of God, *to present your bodies as a living sacrifice*, holy and acceptable to God, which is your spiritual worship.
>
> ROMANS 12:1, NRSV, EMPHASIS ADDED

The background of this rich imagery is the Jewish sacrificial system. Only here, Paul calls believers not to offer a sacrificial animal to

God but instead to present, offer, *surrender* our bodies—our lives—to him for his use, no matter the cost. This release of control, this turning over of everything that is us—our hopes, dreams, relationships, resources, health, and destiny—to God, is the primary way we're called to worship him. But here's what I don't want you to miss: According to Paul, our motivation to surrender isn't simply that God is God, sovereign and all-powerful—but rather because of his many "mercies."

What are these mercies? God saw us in our sin and rebellion (Romans 1:18-32) and remarkably, instead of responding with rejection and judgment, moved toward us with compassion and mercy most specifically and powerfully displayed in his love for us through Jesus Christ: "The *love* of God has been poured out in our hearts," Paul writes (Romans 5:5, emphasis added). And then, a few verses later, "God demonstrates His own *love* toward us, in that while we were still sinners, Christ died for us" (Romans 5:8, emphasis added). Finally, at the end of Romans 8, Paul pens one of the most heart-gripping, hope-filled paragraphs about the endless mercy of God's love for us in all of history:

> Who shall separate us from the *love* of Christ? Shall tribulation, or distress, or persecution, or famine, or nakedness, or peril, or sword? . . . Yet in all these things we are more than conquerors through Him who *loved* us. For I am persuaded that neither death nor life, nor angels nor principalities nor powers, nor things present nor things to come, nor height nor depth, nor any other created thing, shall be able to separate us from the *love* of God which is in Christ Jesus our Lord.
>
> ROMANS 8:35, 37-39, EMPHASIS ADDED

This is why we surrender—because of the illogical, undeserved, recklessly generous *mercies* of God toward us, especially the mercy of a love that will not fail us, despite the number of times we fail the One who gives it. Even if our lives spiral out of control or the world around us comes crashing down—because we trust his merciful love, we yield our circumstances and sometimes even our next breath to him. Surrender doesn't guarantee a pain-free journey: "In the world you will have tribulation," Jesus warned (John 16:33). But his love, even in the darkness, remains faithful. Julian of Norwich, witness to the Black Death that killed half of Europe's population, said so profoundly:

> If there be any lover of God on earth who is continuously kept from falling, I do not know of it, for it was not shown to me. But this was shown: that in falling and rising *we are always tenderly protected in one love.*[6]

Now, you may be thinking, *Don't proponents of "just do it" Christianity also call us to surrender?* "God is our creator and ruler," they remind us. "He commands us to yield to his authority and might be justly annoyed and withhold blessing—even discipline us— if we don't." There's a key difference between this kind of surrender and what we're talking about. "Surrender because you should . . . and because you're afraid" are the same reasons the ancients bowed before Zeus and the pantheon of fickle Greco-Roman gods. Not only does this picture misrepresent our God, but obligation and fear as motivation for surrender are unsustainable. Eventually, we weary of bowing the knee because we're guilt-ridden, intimidated, or afraid—and we give up. In fact, long before that point, even while we're surrendering on the surface, deep in our hearts, we're hedging our bets and obsessing about backup plans, just in case our trust in God doesn't get us the results we want.

Paul well knew of God's magnificent, sovereign authority—"of Him and through Him and to Him are all things, to whom be glory forever" (Romans 11:36). But he's crystal clear about why he lives surrendered: "I live by faith in the Son of God, who *loved* me and gave Himself for me" (Galatians 2:20, emphasis added). No one abides apart from surrender—and no one consistently surrenders without knowing and trusting God's love.

Some of us are saying, "Got it. So, what are the steps to surrendering? Give me a list of things to do, something tangible that will assure me I'm doing it right." I would if I could. But surrender isn't about lists and steps. Surrender is simply our heart's response to the God whose love secures us. It's unclenching our fists and releasing whatever we've been gripping out of fear—a cherished relationship, difficult situation, or confusing decision—into the loving, capable hands of a God who is our Father. Surrender is relinquishing control . . . to our One Great Love.

And remember, surrender isn't a one-shot proposition—it's a moment-by-moment act of worship, as necessary to abiding as breathing is to living. Yesterday's yielding of control is powerful for yesterday's battle—but today's fresh challenge calls for a renewed "Lord, all I am and have is yours." A few weeks after my pivotal moment of surrender, one of Hope's pastors, Rita Beale, who hadn't been to our home in several years, "happened" to stop by one afternoon just as we received another call about Carla's elusive diagnosis. Just as our world came crashing down around us . . . again.

Several labs had been struggling to identify the specific cancer invading Carla's thyroid, and a hospital nurse called us with their tentative conclusion—a cancer neither of us had heard of before.

Ignoring Carla's "please no," I immediately consulted Wikipedia, and what I read buckled my knees.

"Carla"—my voice trembled—"you need to sit down because the news isn't good." I drew her close and reluctantly, tenderly, honestly whispered the truth of what seemed like a death sentence. My best friend collapsed in my arms, and I sobbed, "Father, please, please be with us. We're so afraid, and we don't know what to do." After a few moments, we stumbled to the living room where I had surrendered Carla weeks earlier, and with Pastor Rita holding us and crying out to God on our behalf, I surrendered the love of my life . . . again.

I wasn't done. After even more testing, we eventually received Carla's final diagnosis—a cancer so rare that our expert team at the University of Michigan Medical Center was forced to piece together Carla's treatment plan from best-practice protocols—calling me to surrender her again. Then, when they wheeled her into surgery down that long corridor, doors ominously closing one by one behind her, I tearfully surrendered her again. Sitting in the surgery waiting area for four hours while Carla lay with her throat open a few rooms away, I entrusted her to my Abba again. When we walked into the medical center for her first chemotherapy treatment, I wept because I so desperately wanted to take her place—but instead, I released her to the Father's arms again. And then waiting in our surgeon's office for our first PET scan results and the second and the third . . . each time I surrendered her—yet again—to my One Great Love.

The reality is, if I want any peace or power or freedom, I must also surrender—moment by moment—Andrea, Leigh Anne, and Caroline, Dusty and John, Ada, Mack, Van, and little Johnny—all of whom I love beyond words and am terribly frightened to lose. I must surrender precious, lifelong friends who are like brothers and sisters; aging parents and extended family; my own aging body; our precarious finances; our ministry to pastors and their families; our home, cars, and possessions; my past, present, and future. Everyone. Everything. With every breath, I'm compelled by the mercies of God to present my body—my life—as a living sacrifice to the One who has promised to always keep me in his love.

Because here's the raw truth: Either we surrender, or all we have left is *the illusion of control*. As I've written this book, a rogue microbe has brought the mighty nations of the world to their knees—including our own powerful, prosperous United States. In a flash, our optimistic future, gone. Our ability to plan, gone. Our mobility, gone. Job and financial security, gone. Stock-market gains, gone. Confidence that good genes, exercise, diet, and robust health coverage guarantees long life, gone. Even our ability to try and keep the illusion of control afloat with schedules, school, vacations, restaurants, the gym, professional sports, family reunions, and church activities—gone. In an unforeseen instant—all of it, gone. The control we depended so much on for our security, joy, and hope has been outed as the imposter it always was. We're left with only two real choices—the same two choices the embattled, severely challenged people of God have faced throughout history: either surrender to a God who promises that his love for us is stronger than hell itself—or stay in the land of "I'm on my own," a land also called "fear and despair."

As I close this chapter, martyred Archbishop Óscar Romero of El Salvador is on my mind. In 1977, Romero's close friend, Jesuit priest Rutilio Grande, courageous advocate for the persecuted poor, was murdered by the ruling elite in escalating conflict between the wealthy and El Salvador's marginalized masses. Up until that time, Romero was considered conservative, reserved, even afraid to get involved in his country's class struggle, but his friend's murder broke his heart and poured resolve into his spirit. If standing for

Christ with the poor led to his friend's death, "then I too have to walk the same path," Romero said.[7] Just days later, brokenhearted and disheveled, Archbishop Romero stumbled alone to the dusty, countryside intersection where Father Grande had been assassinated. Frightened but resolute, he collapsed, face toward glory, and cried out to his God,

"I can't. You must. I'm yours. Show me the way."[8]

That prayer of surrender established Romero's life of abiding in Jesus over the next two years of violent conflict with the powers of darkness in El Salvador. Surrender enveloped and protected his spirit on a March evening in 1980 when he held high the body of his Christ during Mass at a hospital for the terminally ill—and a sniper's bullet pierced his heart. I've prayed his prayer of surrender hundreds of times in the last twenty-five years, and I'm silently offering my Jesus these words today as I wrestle with anxiety during the pandemic: *Father, so much need, pain, and uncertainty—even about my own health. I can't. You must. I'm yours. Show me the way.*

Remember, surrender is never about results we can see or even results we desire. My wife Carla, according to her recent PET scan, is cancer free! On the other hand, Archbishop Romero, despite the surrendered prayers of many, was martyred. We don't surrender because we're guaranteed positive earthly outcomes. We surrender because of his mercies, especially the mercy of his love. We surrender because letting go sets us free—free from the need to live in a fearful prison of present aloneness or future what-ifs. We know that when we abide in his love—a love that nothing in heaven or earth can separate us from—then even if he doesn't deliver us from the fiery furnace, the lions' den, or the cross, we can still say with David, and the Son of

David, "Into Your hand I commit my spirit . . . You are my God. My times are in Your hand" (Psalm 31:5, 14-15; Luke 23:46).

Are you tired of living in the land of "I'm on my own"—the land of insecure, anxious bondage to the next set of circumstances life brings your way? Have courage, my friend. Lift your heart, gaze at the compassionate face of Jesus, and see his eyes full of love . . . for you. Then, take your life—your relationships, circumstances, and plans you've been trying with all your strength to control—and surrender it to God as a living sacrifice. With your brother Oscar Romero and millions of believers in history, say to God, "I can't. You must. I'm yours. Show me the way." I know you're scared. I'm scared too. Take my hand, and together, let's begin *right now*—in this moment—to choose the freedom and power of the abiding life.

Chapter 5

WITH ME

Be sure of this: I am with you always, even to the end of the age.

MATTHEW 28:20, NLT

*Please, don't leave me, don't leave me, Jesus. Don't leave, don't leave me,
Lord. . . . I don't believe that God would bring me this far just to leave me.*

CURTIS BURRELL

Fear not for mighty dread, cause I'll be there at your side.

BOB MARLEY

**Abiding in Jesus' love calls us to learn
to trust that he is truly always near.**

*WHAT I PROMISE IS THAT I LOVE YOU, I will be with you, and I will never
leave you. Ever.*

Words I heard God speak to my anxious heart that first afternoon
when I finally turned toward him after days of angry silence. Words
that ultimately moved me to surrender my best friend in her battle
with cancer. I understood he wasn't going to guarantee that Carla
would survive—he's not a genie in a bottle, after all. And I understood we don't get to know the future. But if I was going to make
my home in his love on the long, arduous journey ahead, I needed
desperately to know *my Father loved us and was going to be with us
every step of the way.* Because in the valley of the shadows, we don't
find security in results—but in his loving presence.

73

"I will fear no evil, because you—my loving shepherd—are with me," David says (Psalm 23:4, author's paraphrase). This truth that God loves us and is always with us is so crucial to our abiding in him in our broken, hostile world that his presence is both promised and revealed repeatedly in the biblical story. In the post-captivity wilderness, God is visibly with his people in a cloud by day and a pillar of fire at night (Exodus 13:21). On the banks of the Jordan River, as anxious Israel stares into the daunting Promised Land, God comforts her, "Take courage. . . . GOD, your God, is . . . right there with you. He won't let you down; he won't leave you" (Deuteronomy 31:6, MSG). King Solomon built the Temple in the capital city of Jerusalem, where God lived among his people (1 Kings 8:10-13). When Israel looked toward the Temple in times of stress or danger, they knew their God was near.

And then, there's Jesus Christ. Immanuel—God with us (Matthew 1:23). On the last night of his earthly life, his Kingdom mission almost fulfilled, he reassures his panicky disciples—now in charge—"The Father . . . will give you another Helper, that He may abide *with* you forever—the Spirit of truth . . . you know Him, for He dwells *with* you and will be in you. I will not leave you orphans; I will come to you" (John 14:16-18, emphasis added). Then, after the Resurrection, moments before he crosses into glory, Jesus declares to this same frightened group, "Be sure of this: I am *with you* always, even to the end of the age" (Matthew 28:20, NLT, emphasis added).

God spoke that same encouraging promise to me that life-altering afternoon. But in the days ahead, as Carla and I began having scary conversations with surgeons and oncologists, a question emerged—a question I've often wondered if the disciples pondered, as well: *What exactly did Jesus mean when he said he would be with us?* Clearly, at least that he would be with us—and in us—through the presence of the Holy Spirit (John 14:16-18).[1] Comforting indeed. But in the storm we were in, I longed to be assured that the Jesus who invited me to abide in his love would be right beside us—in his resurrected body—as we walked into the darkness of cancer. So, was that his promise? Or was he promising to be with us only in some metaphorical, spiritual, cosmic, "I've got the whole world in my hands" kind of way? Because if *that* is what he was saying, it wasn't going to be enough. Like David of old, if I was going to abide in the love of Jesus while journeying through the valley of the shadow of death, I had to know my shepherd was right . . . by . . . my . . . side.

So what *did* Jesus mean when he said, "I am with you always" (Matthew 28:20)? What I believed before Carla's cancer is that when Jesus ascended into heaven (Luke 24:51; Acts 1:9), he flew to a mystical destination called "the right hand of the Father," likely a few light-years away. If that was where Jesus set up shop, then his promise of "nearness" really was a figure of speech. But my longing for his *real presence* compelled me to rethink this view. With help from N. T. Wright,[2] I began to wonder if heaven wasn't "out there"—but rather right here, beside me, in another dimension across a thin spiritual veil that separates earth from glory. This would explain how after the Resurrection, one moment Jesus was with the disciples, and then was gone—then with two of his followers on the road to Emmaus, and then gone. He was simply moving back and forth between heaven and earth (John 20:19-29; Luke 24:13-35).

And what if the heavenly right hand of the Father, the position of honor and power from which, Paul says, Jesus prays for us, isn't in a far-off corner of the universe, but instead is very, very near (Romans 8:34)? What if during spiritual battle, when shells are exploding all around and we're bleeding out and all seems lost—what if we can know that Jesus of Nazareth, the resurrected Lord, is literally with us?

What if our trust in and experience of his actual nearness and presence are intended to sustain us in the abiding life?

I think this is exactly what Paul is getting at in his oft-quoted words to the Philippian church: "Do not worry about anything" (Philippians 4:6). Usually we quickly move on to what Paul says next about prayer as an antidote for worry. But notice what happens if you include the last phrase in verse 5 with verses 6 through 8:

> *The Lord is near.* Do not worry about anything, but in everything by prayer and supplication with thanksgiving let your requests be made known to God. And the peace of God, which surpasses all understanding, will guard your hearts and your minds in Christ Jesus.
>
> PHILIPPIANS 4:5-8, NRSV, EMPHASIS ADDED

The phrase "the Lord is near" changes everything! Paul could be alluding to the "near" return of Jesus at the end of the age, but I think it's even more likely he's referring to Jesus' promise to be *near us right now* in a way that secures us when we feel threatened, worried, and afraid.[3] Paul calls us to pray—to cry out to a God who isn't far off but, in the person of the Lord Jesus, is very, very near. Otherworldly peace is promised not because of specific answers to our prayers but because of the transcendent reality that wherever we are, whatever we're going through, the Lord Jesus who promised to be with us always . . . is. He is near, surrounding us with his protective, abiding love. These words weren't theory to Paul. Years later, in the last days of his own life, facing execution alone in a Roman prison, Paul writes, "Everyone abandoned me. . . . But the Lord stood *with me* and gave me strength" (2 Timothy 4:16-17, NLT, emphasis added). In other words, any minion of hell who wants a piece of a son or daughter of God must first fight through the Lion of Judah (Revelation 5:5), who stands by our side.

Remember Stephen—the first Christian martyr? After his long and passionate public defense of Jesus as Messiah, a furious mob of religious leaders thronged to stone him as a blasphemer. At that precise moment, the heavens opened, and Stephen saw "the Son of Man standing at the right hand of God"—not far off, but very near, *with him* in the terrifying darkness (Acts 7:56). In the most agonizing, horrific moments of his life, Stephen courageously stands his ground . . . and when the end comes, he speaks directly to Jesus—"Lord Jesus, receive my spirit"—as if held safely, securely in his arms, gazing into the loving eyes of the One who promised to never, ever leave him alone.

Listen carefully: Stephen wasn't a superhero. He was human, just like you and me. He was victorious in his battle with the powers of darkness because he lived abiding in the love of a Jesus he knew was literally *with him*—not just in good health and prosperity but in the barren, treacherous wilderness as well. So it is with us. We can't just hope, guess, or theorize that Jesus is near when the enemy launches financial challenge, relational conflict, emotional pain, and other kinds of death our way. In the crucial hour of spiritual battle, like Stephen, we must *know* that Jesus Christ is by our side with a love hell itself cannot defeat. Otherwise, when danger appears on the horizon, we'll find ourselves looking for the nearest exit.

I remember the morning Carla and I walked, hand in hand, into the University of Michigan Cancer Center for her first day of chemotherapy and radiation. Tears come to my eyes even now as I relive that sacred moment—but the truth is, I was very afraid. Carla felt differently. "I wanted to have a good attitude and was so grateful we were finally doing something to kill any remaining cancer," she reminisced recently. "At one point, I do remember being really scared to lose my hair! But that morning, I was amazingly calm about everything." Fair enough—but I was petrified.

The medical staff had been so genuinely caring, kind, and professional—encouraging us in so many ways and pledging their undying support through the grueling, three-month process to come. Nevertheless, my mind was swamped with uncertainties I couldn't control. Would Carla be overcome by devastating nausea from the cancer-destroying poison infused into her system? Would radiation intended to burn away any remaining cancer cells in Carla's neck damage good tissue as well? This cancer was so rare—would the treatment protocols even work? What about long-term impact on Carla's immune system? Would she be riddled with months of worry? More importantly, would my friend and love be able to trust her heavenly Father's goodness—the same Father who had allowed his daughter to contract this strange, extraordinarily rare cancer in the first place? All this and so much more overwhelmed me early that morning as Carla and I slowly found our way to her appointment with healing.

But remarkably, anxiety wasn't my only companion. I can't really explain how I knew—but Jesus was near. Of course, I didn't see and hear him as I might see and hear a friend over a cup of coffee. Nevertheless, the reality of his presence was substantial, striking, certain. It was as if he walked between us—one arm around Carla's shoulders and his other arm around mine. As we passed by fellow strugglers on crutches, in wheelchairs, some who had lost hair, weight, and limbs—and some who seemed to have lost hope—it was as if Jesus pulled me close, nodded his head in the direction of the others, and whispered, "I've got you and Carla. Why don't you spend some time this morning praying for them?" It was one of the most remarkable moments of my life. His loving presence secured me in my insecurity—even while giving me courage to let go of my self-absorption for a moment and partner with him on behalf of the brokenness all around.

Before that exceptional morning, I'm not sure how I would have defined the peace of God. Since that day, I know for sure it isn't the absence of fear but instead trust in—and often, a profound awareness of—the actual presence of Jesus. As Jesus himself said, "These things I have spoken to you, that *in Me* you may have peace" (John 16:33, emphasis added). Now I know that peace isn't a spiritual commodity shipped to us like an Amazon package from some distant corner of the universe if we pray hard enough or read enough Bible verses. In fact, peace isn't a commodity at all. Peace is himself. Peace is his certain presence in the valley of the shadows, letting us know that because of his powerful love, the darkness cannot, will not win. "In the world you will have tribulation," Jesus promised, "but be of good cheer, I have overcome the world" (John 16:33).

But it's true, isn't it, that our knowledge, let alone our felt experience of the presence of Jesus is often at best . . . elusive? Right now, some of you might wish you could reach through the pages of this chapter and ask through tears of frustration, "Why wasn't he near when I lost my job? Why didn't he show up for me when I went through my divorce? Why couldn't I feel him when my son died? Is there some kind of exclusive 'feel Jesus near' club I don't know about, or some special menu of spiritual achievements to check off in order to qualify for Jesus showing up—when I've got nothing left? I'm glad for you, Kev, but why doesn't Jesus ever break through the veil . . . for me?"

My brother or sister—right about now, if we were having coffee or taking a walk . . . I wouldn't say much. I'd simply embrace you—and maybe tell you how sorry I am that you've so often felt alone when you needed to feel the presence of Jesus the most. The truth is, I have no easy answers—but I might have some perspective.

For every story of experiencing the presence of Jesus like I did that monumental morning at the cancer center, I have ten others where he's called me to simply trust that he is near. "We walk by faith, not by sight," Paul says (2 Corinthians 5:7). As I shared earlier, I've struggled for a few months with some physical symptoms that have caused me a lot of anxiety—partly because here in Detroit, in the middle of a pandemic, it's not prudent to go into an already swamped medical system to even get checked out. Every morning, I beg the Lord to meet me in my fear in a clearly discernible way like he did that first day of Carla's treatment—to tangibly let me know he is near. And . . . crickets.

But just because I can't "feel" Jesus this time around doesn't mean he isn't actually very, very close. When ancient Israel felt abandoned and alone, she would often stop and *remember* specific times God drew near in the past (Psalm 77:11; 78:1-8)—a *remembering* that is crucial to our encouragement as well, especially when all seems dark. But other times, I'm convinced he's asking me—and maybe you—to grow up and learn to trust that when he said, "I will be with you always," he meant it.

As for an exclusive hyper-spiritual club? No way. I understand why some of us might think that—especially if we've been raised in a performance-based, "just do it" version of Christianity. But it's a lie. Jesus' promise to be near isn't just for the spiritual elite—but for everyone. I do think, however, that in any healthy relationship, increased trust elicits increased personal disclosure. One time when we were dating, I asked Carla why she seemed a little distant. She said, "You know those other girls you occasionally go out with? Drop them. And I promise—I'll come closer." Similarly, just a few paragraphs before Jesus' invitation to his disciples to abide, he said,

> Those who accept my commandments and obey them are the ones who love me. . . . And I will love them and *reveal* myself to each of them.
>
> JOHN 14:21, NLT, EMPHASIS ADDED

Let me be clear: Jesus is *not* saying his love is conditional. What he *is* saying is that he deeply desires to show his love for us *by revealing more and more of himself* to us—but that kind of transparency is reserved for those who show by their loving obedience that they can be trusted.[4] That he is *the One* we love. In C. S. Lewis's *Prince Caspian*, Lucy heard and saw Aslan first not because she was his favorite or somehow better than the other children but because of her love for Aslan, so that when he called, she "woke up out of the deepest sleep you can imagine, with the feeling that the voice she liked best in the world had been calling her name."[5]

The other day, I took a long walk and checked in with my friend Cindy, whom I thought might be feeling the impact of the month-long Michigan coronavirus lockdown. When she picked up the phone, I said, "Cindy, this is Pastor Kevin! How are you doing living alone during these crazy, difficult days?" Her reply was immediate and persuasive, "I'm not alone, Pastor. *Jesus is with me!*" You've got to know Cindy to understand that she wasn't kidding or speaking in spiritual metaphor or bragging—she was simply stating her reality. She wasn't alone. She wasn't depressed. She wasn't afraid. Because to Cindy, Jesus was actually . . . with her, by her side. But here's the deal—that's because Jesus is everything to her. She's not like many of us, who treat him as an acquaintance until life gets hard—and *then* we long to feel his presence. Cindy spent forty years on the streets of Detroit as a prostitute and heroin addict, and Jesus literally saved her life, telling her she was going to die if she didn't get clean, staying with her while she detoxed for three days in a locked hotel room, and then speaking forgiveness and freedom to her heart through the Cross.[6] Jesus' voice is the voice Cindy likes best in all the world. Jesus reveals his presence to Cindy in clearer, more consistent ways than to almost anyone I've ever known—because he trusts her. But I also think that on the days when she struggles to sense he is near—*she has learned to trust him.*

There's yet one more reason some of us struggle to "feel" the presence of Jesus: We haven't given ourselves permission to feel much of anything at all. "Pour out your heart before Him," David beckons (Psalm 62:8). But how difficult this is for those of us who have been taught that in our walk with God, feelings themselves are inferior and insignificant compared to discipline, effort, and performance. That was the case with my friend Abby, a vivacious, gifted twenty-year-old I met a few years back in a class I was teaching at Ecola Bible College on the Oregon coast. One evening we sat down at Mo's Seafood and Chowder on the water, and she told me her story:

> I'm the oldest of seven kids raised in a missionary pastor's home, and I've spent my whole life following the rules. I attended church several times a week, and by the time I graduated from high school, I'd read the Bible through at least four times. I still read it every morning—I'm supposed to, right? But I'm bored stiff. The truth is, Pastor Kevin, though I've tried everything to feel close to God—I don't. In fact, I've spent my first twenty years trying to be the tough one—keeping everyone else's spirits up and bottling hurts

from friends and when I did feel something painful, telling myself I needed to stop being a baby and get over it. So deep inside, I not only don't feel God or his love for me—I simply . . . don't . . . feel. So, what do I do?

Sound like anyone you know? Maybe Abby's heart that evening reflects your own frustrated heart just now. If so, listen carefully. "Abby," I said tenderly, "it's time to get alone—and maybe for the first time in your life, have a real talk with God. Tell him your truth. Shout, scream—pour your heart out to him. Let him know how you feel . . . about everything. Don't hold anything back, even if you're angry, even if you say things you never thought you could say to God. He loves you. He's your Father. He can handle it. In fact, I promise you—he's been waiting for this moment for a long, long time."

The next day, Abby wandered in the gray Oregon drizzle to the underside of a nearby bridge, where she turned an emotional corner with her God. "At first, words weren't coming," she told me later. "Then I said, 'God,' and with surprising difficulty, 'Father.' But it was when I muttered, 'I'm angry' that the fountain erupted. For the first time in my life, *I allowed myself to feel with God.* I was screaming and crying, 'Why have you always been so distant? I've tried so hard to be close to you. And yet, I feel nothing. What's wrong with me? Please show me you love me and care for me. Please.'"

Don't miss this: The first time Abby allowed herself to feel with God . . . is the first time she felt God's presence with her—"a calming peace came over me," she said. And then, deep in her spirit, she heard his voice: *Abby, I see your heart. You've always tried to be strong, but you need me. Let me help you.*

Abby said, "In the past, whenever I pictured God, it was with his back to me. He was too busy helping the neglected, hurting people in the world to tend to the 'good kid.' But that day, for the first time in my life, I felt like God looked right at me. It was his tender, loving gaze—focused not just on the world but on me, his daughter—that finally broke through." You know what else Abby told me as we reminisced about that life-changing afternoon? As she poured out her heart to God, she finally felt released from the pressure to perform.

A few years ago, Carla and I took two of our grandsons to a Pioneer Days extravaganza on the grounds of an old ranch near their home outside Denver. Hay wagons and ponies to ride; goats, rabbits, and llamas to pet—Mack and Van thought they'd landed in heaven. And then three-year-old Mack saw the man with the snake. "Papa, I'm not going to touch that snake because I'm afraid," Mack advised me as he began walking rapidly across the expansive green lawn . . . toward the snake. Hurrying to catch up, I reassured him, "You don't have to touch the snake, son. But maybe we can get close enough to look." On the way, several more times he gazed up at me, saying, "I'm not going to touch the snake, Papa, okay?" and each time I smiled and said that's fine.

In a few moments, we arrived at the small booth where the owner was holding his snake safely so that those who wished could risk a touch. Mack stood just a few feet away—and I could tell he really, really wanted to overcome his fear. So I gently suggested, "Hey buddy, *I'm your Papa, and I'm right here with you*—so what if you put your hand on my hand . . . and we touch the snake together?" Wide-eyed, he laid his tiny palm on the back of my protective Papa hand—and together, Mack and his Papa—we touched that snake.

What a moment. Mack was ecstatic! I was so proud of him, but I will never, ever forget what happened next. I about-faced for an instant to invite Carla and Van to celebrate our victory, and when I turned back around, Mack was courageously touching that snake . . . all by himself.

Lizz Wright sings, "I have finally found a place to live, in the presence of the Lord."[7] Just like little Mack with his strong Papa, we long to live in that place—where when we're afraid, even then we can still experience the powerful, comforting presence of our Jesus. Where even when we can't feel Jesus, we're still able to trust that he is with us. This place is crucial to consistently abiding in his protective love. But where to begin? Especially for those already discouraged and worn out from hours of Bible reading, sermon listening, and worship-music playing—strategies meant to keep the fear and darkness at bay, but which sometimes still leave us wondering if Jesus is truly near.

This I can tell you—if you're going to learn to live in the presence of the Lord, it's going to be a fight. Paul calls it "a life-or-death fight to the finish against the Devil and all his angels" (Ephesians 6:10-12, MSG). Because if there's anything the enemy does *not* want you to know about, experience, or trust, it is the nearness of Jesus Christ the King—and the truth that not only does he love you deeply and would never, for any reason in heaven or on earth, leave you alone but also that the powers of darkness themselves cannot keep him from your side. Satan knows that if *you* know, deep in your spirit, that the crucified, risen Jesus loves you and is with you, then there's nothing you can't face in his name. Cancer, drug addiction, lifelong struggle to "feel," martyrdom—even childhood snakes and their adult equivalent—won't be able to separate you from the powerful, protective presence of Jesus and his love.

Maybe all you've got today is a desperate longing to know he's near and a thimbleful of faith. It's enough. "Pour out your heart to him" (Psalm 62:8, NLT). Boldly and bravely, tell him everything. That he is your One Great Love, that you miss him terribly, that you ache for his presence—and that by his grace, you will learn to trust he is with you, even when all you see and feel around you is darkness.

Henri Nouwen was a psychologist, priest, and author who loved Jesus deeply yet sometimes struggled to know he was near. When Nouwen felt alone, this was his heart's cry:

> I call to you, O Lord, from my quiet darkness. Show me your mercy and love. Let me see your face, hear your voice, touch the hem of your cloak. I want to love you, be with you, speak to you, and simply stand in your presence. But I cannot make it happen. Pressing my eyes against my hands is not praying and reading about your presence is not living in it.
>
> But there is that moment in which you will come to me, as you did to your fearful disciples, and say, "Do not be afraid; it is I." Let that moment come soon, O Lord. And if you want to delay it, then make me patient. Amen.[8]

A prayer for the abiding life.

Chapter 6

MYSTERY AND THE LOVE OF JESUS

Jesus Christ, whom having not seen you love.

I PETER 1:7-8

You, God, who live next door—
If at times, through the long night, I trouble you
with my urgent knocking—
this is why: I hear you breathe so seldom. . . .
I wait listening, always. Just give me a sign!

RAINER MARIA RILKE

Abiding in Jesus' love calls us to surrender our demand for certainty and learn to allow God's love to sustain us even in the darkness of mystery.

I WAS RAISED IN A CHRISTIANITY that provided "solid" answers—*to all questions.* The Bible was a spiritual textbook, complete with a topical index of verses referencing every subject imaginable. We were rightly taught that the overall theme of Scripture is the story of God and his dealings with humans in history—but we were also told it was a story with absolutely no loopholes. In fact, to imply that in some places the Bible seemed to pose unreconcilable dilemmas was a sure sign we were on our way to denying our faith altogether. Clearly, it was impossible to strongly believe in Jesus while living with unanswered questions about almost anything. I had no idea how much my relationship with Jesus depended on such a tight, impenetrable system of belief until the day I had an intense discussion with my close friend Steve—about doubt.

Both of us were in our twenties, were serious about Jesus, had just enough seminary training to make us dangerous, and loved to talk theology. But Steve was more comfortable holding seemingly contradictory perspectives in tension—even calling into question parts of Christianity I considered unquestionable. One day, when we were in the car, our usual theological conversation got heated—mostly, I thought at the time, because Steve wouldn't affirm all my views. In fact, at one point, I got so angry I pounded the dashboard and shouted at God—words I won't repeat here. Then, a few moments later, I added more calmly, "Steve, if I have to wrestle with all these questions, maybe I don't want anything to do with God at all." Looking back, it's clear my frustration wasn't about my friend. I was undone because I had no idea how to believe in Jesus Christ—based on solid historical data and personal experience—while at the same time living with mystery. The thought of mystery in my relationship with God didn't just make me uncomfortable; it scared me to death.

Especially in Western Christianity, we tend to prefer a God who is entirely predictable. That kind of God makes us feel like we're in control. If I press certain keys on my laptop, I know what to expect. We like to think that if we input the right kind of prayers, obedience, and sacrifice, we can be assured of God's reciprocal, no surprises, on-time response. The universe and our lives will work like they're supposed to, with order, predictability, and security. But if that's my view of God and my categories and formulas about him are challenged—I'm not really sure what I have left. And I'm afraid.

But I don't have a relationship with my laptop—so if this is how I connect with God, I don't have much of a relationship with him either. Relationship and control don't mesh. Saying "I love you" never means "I control you" or even "I have you completely figured out." But it does mean "I trust you." When Jesus says, "As the Father has loved me, so have I loved you. Abide in my love"—*he's asking us to trust his love for us*, even in the unpredictable, confusing, sometimes tragically disappointing mystery of life. Even when we can't figure him out. Madame Jeanne Guyon, a well-known serious follower of Jesus in seventeenth-century France, doesn't hold back:

> If knowing answers to life's questions is absolutely necessary to you, then forget the journey. You will never make it, for this is a journey of unknowables—of questions, enigmas, incomprehensibles and most of all, things unfair.[1]

Though much of our faith and how it works out in life is laid out plainly, the mystery of God's dealings with humanity is everywhere in Scripture. Moses refers to the secret things of God (Deuteronomy 29:29). Unanswered questions about what God is doing saturate the lives of the patriarchs, judges, and kings—especially David in the Psalms—and of course, the prophets. Ruth, Esther, and Daniel represent everyday people in Israel trying to trust God in the midst of untimely death, famine, and years of oppressive exile under the domination of Assyria, Babylon, and Persia. The book of Ecclesiastes is filled with questions about the pain and inconsistencies of life, concluding with a call to trust anyway—"Fear God. Do what he tells you. And that's it" (Ecclesiastes 12:13-14, MSG). And then there's the mystery of God becoming human, a virgin mother, miracles, Jesus' cosmic sacrificial death, his dead body alive—walking, talking with his followers—then vanishing into thin air, leaving them with a mystical promise to be with them until his unexplained, undated return.

Peter acknowledges the mystery followers of Jesus live with: "You love him even though you have never seen him. Though you do not see him now, you trust him" (1 Peter 1:8, NLT). Again, Paul adds, "We walk by faith, not by sight" (2 Corinthians 5:7).

Look, I don't pretend to have all the answers about how to live without all the answers. But the Bible is clear—*learning to trust Jesus in the mystery is the only way to truly live in relationship with him.* Otherwise, we begin drifting—often first toward cliché-laden Christianity, which offers quick, inappropriate, and always unhelpful "answers" to the deepest crises and quandaries of life. When we say something like "God must have needed another angel" to a friend who just lost a child, we're not engaging the mystery of tragic death alongside the reality of Jesus' love—but turning our back on the mystery and on relationship with Jesus himself. Because while Jesus lovingly stays near the wounded, clichés launch us to spiritual la-la land, where we hide behind pseudoanswers for deep pain we can't handle.

German philosopher Friedrich Nietzsche said, "In Christianity neither morality nor religion come into contact with reality at any point."[2] One reason nonbelievers reject Christianity is because they see Christians as religious androids who can't handle the truth— especially the harsh reality of pain without answers. To them, we're citizens of *Pleasantville*—clinging desperately to our illusion of a world that always makes sense, hiding behind packaged Christian proverbs and memes because deep inside, we're petrified our faith in Jesus won't survive wounds that can't be explained. Then we invite our hurting friends to put their trust in Jesus and wonder why they respond, "No, thank you very much."

Ironically, many times these clichés are misquoted, out-of-context Bible verses meant to give real comfort! Like "All things work together for good" (Romans 8:28), which isn't a promise of instant visible good out of horrific bad—but the true consolation of knowing that our sovereign Father is constantly transforming our earthly pain into *eternal* good through his powerful love. Sadly, we don't just foist these clichés on others but preach them to ourselves until they become the substance of our shallow Christian lives. Job's rebuke of his cliché-spouting companions says it all: "I've had all I can take of your talk. What a bunch of miserable comforters!" (Job 16:1-5, MSG).

Sometimes, those of us too honest to cling to clichés . . . simply get stuck. I have a close friend who really believes in Jesus and wants to walk more closely with him—but whenever something happens in his personal life or in the broken world around him that he can't reconcile with what he believes about God, he checks out spiritually for a while. Then a few months later, he wanders back, asking, "Can you help me deepen my relationship with Jesus?" If you recognize this pattern in your life, the answer is, *Not until you're willing to wrestle with trusting Jesus and his love in the mystery of pain you don't understand.*

Tragically, there are also those who stop believing altogether. I know a brilliant scientist who gave up his faith not only over intellectual questions about Christianity but also because he was wounded deeply by believers who said they loved him—yet treated him like trash. I have another friend—a former pastor—who left ministry and Christianity after her husband left her and their son for another woman. She told me, "I gave my life to serve God and this is my reward? What kind of God is that?" Listen: I don't judge my brothers and sisters who leave the faith because of trauma. I've already confessed that I'm not sure my faith could survive losing one of my girls. As Buechner notes, "Even Jesus on his cross asked that hardest of questions."[3]

But the travesty is, many who let go of their faith might have survived the mystery of their pain or questions had the church done a better job of creating a safe, welcoming space for their wrestlings and doubt. Remember Thomas? When his faith crashed over the mystery of losing Jesus to a cross, he wasn't shamed and exiled; he stayed with the other disciples, where his broken spirit was loved and nurtured—until Jesus met his doubt *in the community* and healed him (John 20:24-29). Unfortunately, the church is more often like this tweet I saw earlier this morning:

> Church is absolutely a safe space to ask your questions but not too many questions and you had better arrive at the correct answers or you're out and also we'll never speak to you ever again let us pray[4]

So, how does abiding in the love of Jesus help us navigate the darkness of living with all this mystery? I know we're entering sacred and sometimes very personal territory. Some of our most profound wounds and doubts live and breathe in our unanswered questions. I'm asking you to trust that what I share in the pages ahead comes from my deep love for you—and my own heartfelt struggle alongside you.

Consider the mystery of prayer. We've all experienced the sadness and loneliness of heartfelt prayers seemingly left unanswered. Of course, there are a few clues about unanswered prayer in Scripture—and there's always the old standby response: "God is our loving Father, and he gets to make choices about how he responds to his children's requests." Fair enough. But honestly, sometimes these answers just aren't enough—especially for serious followers of Jesus who wonder, *I really don't ask God for that much—couldn't he say yes just this once?*

A few years back, Carla's sister Paula was diagnosed with breast cancer. Paula was an amazing human being—a gifted school counselor; a tenacious advocate of children and of justice for all; and a lover of animals, her husband, and her three children. And she was in love with Jesus. For three years, hundreds of friends and family prayed, coaxed, and begged God to heal his daughter of the cancer ravaging her body. Paula's mother, Sally, had already lost a son (at birth) and her husband (years later, to a drunk driver)—she pleaded daily with God to spare her daughter, standing on various passages of Scripture she believed God himself had given her for comfort. There were prayers accompanied by anointing with oil and the laying on of hands, prayers in groups, prayers soaked in faith that God not only could but would heal his child. But still, Paula died. Why didn't God answer our prayers to heal Paula? Or your similar heartfelt prayers for anything and everything? The truth is—I simply don't know. This I can tell you: It's not your fault. You didn't pray "wrong." Sometimes all we have is the mystery of God saying, "I'm so sorry, daughter. I hate disappointing you, son. I love you with an everlasting love, but have courage—because this time my answer is . . . no."

This, my brothers and sisters, is one reason why Jesus said, "Abide in My love." And why we've spent so much time talking about how to know his personal love for us. Because when God doesn't respond the way we desire, when he breaks our heart by saying no . . . *only confidence in his deep love assures us he is with us even when we're drowning in bitter tears of disappointment.* The day my sister-in-law found out there was nothing else the doctors could do, I sent her a text: "Paula, after today's news, I am praying you will not be afraid." Her reply touched me deeply: "For sure, I am not afraid." A few weeks later, Paula went to be with Jesus. But the truth is, she had been with Jesus all along—even in the darkness of unanswered prayer—safely held in the arms of her One Great Love.

Buechner's historical novel about the life of the twelfth-century holy man Godric of Finchale contains a courageous meditation on the mystery of prayer. Some might find his words too raw—but they've given me great comfort over the years when I've felt over-whelmed by the heartbreak of prayers unanswered:

> What's prayer? It's shooting shafts into the dark. What mark
> they strike, if any, who's to say? It's reaching for a hand you
> cannot touch. The silence is so fathomless that prayers like
> plummets vanish in the sea. You beg. You whimper. You
> load God down with empty praise. You tell him sins that he
> already knows full well. You seek to change his changeless
> will. Yet Godric prays the way he breathes, for else his heart
> would wither in his breast. Prayer is the wind that fills his
> sail. Else waves would dash him on the rocks, or he would
> drift with witless tides. And sometimes, by God's grace, a
> prayer is heard.[5]

And then there's unanswered prayer's mysterious partner—suffering. I first remember experiencing this when my grandmother Lela died. I was nine years old and felt like I'd lost the one person who really saw me. I was overwhelmed by sadness and the mystery of why she had to leave. When I began pastoral ministry twenty years later, suffering was everywhere. So many horrific memories—burying a young mother in a casket with one of her twin sons, both killed in an automobile crash. Officiating the funeral of a baby boy, and a few months later, burying his daddy, who killed himself, over-come by the pain. The suffering of poverty, racial injustice, women mistreated by men, mental illness, abortion, addiction, divorce, child abuse, natural disasters, lost jobs, chronic illness, loneliness, betrayal, and shattered dreams. I've witnessed firsthand the suffer-ing aftermath of civil war in Liberia, apartheid in South Africa, and colonialism in Uganda.

The other day, as we stood helplessly watching a second wave of COVID-19 ravage America, Carla said, "There's really no safe day . . . ever." She's right. In our fallen world, the mystery of suffering is everywhere, devastating all of us—often with no rhyme, reason, or explanation. It must not be rationalized, avoided through cliché, or allowed to crush us in its satanic grip. Followers of Jesus are called to face it head-on, finding comfort and hope in the love of Jesus, who walks with us in our suffering.

But how? In my experience, first we must own that our suffering can't be completely analyzed and figured out. My friend Aubrey Sampson explains,

> Some suffering is the result of sin and the world's brokenness. Other suffering is the result of corrupt leadership. Some suffering we bring on ourselves. *But not all suffering is the* clear result *of something.*[6]

Our friends' four-year-old daughter was recently diagnosed with leukemia. There were no answers. Only mystery. But even when there *are* answers, an element of mystery remains. In the early days of the church, crazy Herod Agrippa persecuted both James and Peter, two of Jesus' closest followers. James was beheaded—while Peter was imprisoned and then miraculously delivered by an angel and celebrated as a hero (Acts 12:1-19). Can you imagine James' mother talking to God? "Tell me what I'm missing here, Lord. Peter's the one who denied Jesus, but he gets rescued? How could you let insane Herod kill my boy? What did my son ever do to you?" Years ago, I officiated the funeral of a young woman who overdosed. There were clear reasons for her death—but still, so much mystery. She did well in rehab, was a serious follower of Jesus, and had great support—what happened?

Could we have done more? Where was God? All torturously unanswerable questions. The mystery of suffering.

Here's the point—we often hide behind analysis to avoid feeling the frightening impact of pain we can't control. Job's friends analyze his pain for thirty biblical chapters! Yes, much of human suffering demands a measure of analysis and corresponding just response, both personally and systemically, to mitigate further pain. This is especially true if we follow Jesus Christ. *But all suffering calls us to lament.* As the psalmist wrote, "Weeping may last through the night, but joy comes with the morning" (Psalm 30:5, NLT). To survive the mystery of suffering, we must sit with our pain and grieve, not to find answers but as Sampson says, "to be still in the unanswerable."[7] Listen carefully—lament is a gift God gives his people, inviting us to take our pain to him and receive his healing in return. It is here, in that sacred space where we sob our suffering and our unanswered questions to our Father while furiously pounding on his chest, that Jesus will meet us with his love and hold us, heal us, and give us courage to go on.

Between 1989 and 2003, Liberia, West Africa, endured two civil wars, resulting in the deaths of hundreds of thousands of Liberians and traumatizing countless others. In 2014, I traveled there with a small group to teach and serve. One afternoon, during a session on the healing power of lament, I paused and asked everyone to contemplate what pain they held on to, and to imagine Jesus, compassionately extending his nail-pierced hands, inviting them to bring their suffering to him. A holy quiet settled in the room. And then, a middle-aged Liberian businessman named Jaa—an inventor, linguist, and Bible translator—sitting two feet away from me . . . began to wail. Seconds turned into minutes as we sat in sacred silence with this precious brother as he poured out his pain to Jesus. Finally, he slowly lifted his head and haltingly said, "I saw horrible things during the war. Gruesome, nightmarish violence I've never told anyone about, death visions that haunt me day and night. I knew Jesus called me to endure suffering. *But I didn't know he could take my suffering.* Today has been a great gift. I'll never be the same." No satisfying answers or explanations from God. Just mysterious, healing love—available to us if we'll pour out our suffering to him.

But there's more. What if we could be assured that Jesus isn't just "there" in our suffering—but that he *suffers with us in our suffering*? Over the years, I've wept with many victims of abuse or other hurt who wondered why Jesus didn't stop the pain and deliver them. Almost always, when I've tearfully explained that everyone—even those who have wounded us—is given a choice to love or hate, heal or abuse . . . they understood. But every time, their next question would torment me: "You say Jesus promised to be with me, so what was he doing while I was being hurt? Standing off to the side—helpless?"

I had no answer. Until one day, when I began to think about Jesus taking our sin onto his body on the cross, "pierced for our rebellion, crushed for our sins . . . beaten so we could be whole . . . whipped so we could be healed" (Isaiah 53:5, NLT). *The Jesus who loves us that much would never, ever stand off to the side while we're being abused.* I began to imagine Jesus wrapping his body around our body even as we're being hurt—physically, verbally, emotionally—one powerful arm extended to ward off our attacker, while shouting, "Stop, now!" Then, if they continue still, *taking the abuse directed toward us first into himself*—as he did on the cross, while whispering to our breaking hearts, "I love you. I've got you. This isn't the end of your story. Your abuser will be dealt with. You . . . will heal. And I will never leave you. Ever."

Listen, I know many of you have been deeply wounded—beyond explanation or understanding. But this I also know: The Son of God who suffered for you on the cross *also suffered with you* when you were hurt—in that broken relationship; at that terrifying, wounding moment; taking the blows, the shame, the betrayal, the violation into his own body. He was there with you. For you. Because he loves you. He is still with you now, sharing your pain even as he heals your pain, all the way to glory.

One more profound mysterious truth about this mystery. If we abide in his love, *suffering does not win.* As you know, this side of heaven, Satan has a long rope. There's a reason he's called the present "ruler of this world" (John 12:31, ESV). One day he'll be deposed, but until then, his goal is to destroy us—often through the devastation of suffering. For those who depend on a Christianity built primarily on tight belief systems and exhaustive answers for protection and power: good luck. But those who abide in the powerful love of Jesus Christ can count on God taking the suffering intended to destroy them—and cramming it back down the enemy's throat.

In Susan Bergman's *Martyrs,* Barbara Lazear Ascher tells the story of Eva Price, young mother of two and a missionary to China during the days of the Boxer Rebellion. In human terms, the mission was a disaster. Eva lost everything—including, in the end, her life. But as Ascher poured over Eva's personal letters from those traumatic years, she noticed that something more powerful than suffering was afoot:

> Eva's . . . heart, in breaking, broke open.
>
> Having lost two children, the support of family, the proximity of friends, thus stripped to her soul by the fires of suffering, she began to sense that *she was supported by a mysterious love that emerges from ashes.* In turn, she was able to love expansively. Suffering breaks us open to grace. . . .
>
> . . . It is only when the heart has been split open that the truths of Christianity can flow in.[8]

This reminds me of Paul, who at one point described his own life as an experience of being "crushed and overwhelmed beyond our ability to endure" (2 Corinthians 1:8, NLT)—and then penned these mysterious, unbelievably hope-filled words:

> We do not lose heart. . . . For our light affliction, which is but for a moment, is working for us a far more exceeding and eternal weight of glory.
> 2 CORINTHIANS 4:16-17

I'm thinking of my dear friend Audrey, who has been battling multiple sclerosis for the last twenty years, or my sister Anitra, who recently lost her precious son, or my brother pastor Prince Mntambo, who endured decades of South Africa's apartheid. All have experienced unbelievable, unexplainable suffering—yet all continue to love Jesus with everything they have and live with a depth of character and compassion realized by few. I have no explanation—except that *when our lives are saturated in the love of Jesus Christ, suffering cannot win.* Wounded brothers and sisters, I know this truth doesn't take away your pain. But I'm praying you will be increasingly aware that as you walk with Jesus, something greater than suffering is afoot in your life too. His love, in your pain, is birthing glory.

Before we finish, the greatest mystery of all—death—deserves a word. Albert King sings, "Everybody wants to go to heaven, / But nobody wants to die,"[9] reminding us how uncomfortable we are and how many questions we have about leaving this life for the next. How will death come to us? Slowly or quickly, painfully or peacefully? Will we be surrounded by love or die alone? And what about heaven—does it exist? If so, what is it like, and am I going there?

The reality is death and eternity are dripping with mystery, primarily because we haven't yet experienced death ourselves—or been to the other side. Whatever we believe can't be about what we've seen—but what we're trusting to be true. So we look to Scripture, which, truth be told, says much more about following Jesus in this life and bringing God's Kingdom to earth now than it does about death and the afterlife. Nevertheless, *what Scripture does say about dying and eternity is powerful.* Jesus himself makes an astounding claim at the death of his friend Lazarus—one which, if true, changes literally everything:

> I am the resurrection and the life. Anyone who believes in me will live, even after dying. Everyone who lives in me and believes in me will never ever die.
>
> JOHN 11:25-26, NLT

Words still drenched with mystery. But words I hang on to not because I totally understand them—*but because Jesus said them.* The One who loves me. The One history says was crucified for the forgiveness of my sins. And the One who came out of the grave, demonstrating that death itself was finally . . . dead.†

But the reason I'm not afraid to die isn't because I can definitively prove anything about the empty tomb or the afterlife. *It's because my relationship with Jesus is more real to me than anything else in this world.*

Truth about Jesus only has value if it leads us to connect deeply and intimately with him as a real person. I used to scoff at the lyrics of a hymn that claimed, "You ask me how I know he lives? / He lives within my heart."¹⁰ I scoff no more. Now, my relationship with

---

† Every major sermonic presentation of the good news of Jesus in Acts, the history of the early church, rests on this reality—"God raised Jesus from the dead, and we are all witnesses" (Acts 2:32, NLT). Without the resurrection, his followers had only his teaching and a few miracles—amazing stuff, yet still only words and deeds to be compared with every other philosopher, sage, and prophet in history. It's also crucial to note that the Roman and Jewish authorities never found his body when they had great motivation to do so—a dead Jesus presented no threat, but a Jesus even thought to be alive was trouble for both political Rome and Israel.

him—and his love—is everything. We cannot navigate the intimidating mysteries of death and eternity by simply trying harder to believe all the appropriate Bible verses or by reading all the best books on the subject. Ultimately, our freedom to live powerfully for Jesus Christ, surrounded by these mysteries, depends on the depth of our love relationship with him.

So, when my daughter Andrea came to me a few years back, asking, "Hey, Dad, heaven freaks me out a little—I understand how cool it will be to live on a new earth and be able to explore and create and connect with millions of people . . . but forever? We're so used to endings and beginnings, how can anything be good . . . if it never ends?" I told her I understood and often wondered the same thing! I think I even shared C. S. Lewis's thoughts about uncomfortability with time being a sure sign we're destined to live outside of it.[11] But then I said, "Andrea, you believe Jesus loves you and gave his life so you could be with him forever. Will you trust him to make eternity a place of joy and freedom, not frustration?" I didn't offer foolproof answers to the mysteries of life and death and following Jesus. There are none. I can only point to Jesus—because as we face unanswerable questions, *our security must come from him.*

So many other questions surround this mystery—and the answer is always the same.

> *Will I go to heaven even though I've messed up so much?* Jesus promises you eternal life—if you'll simply believe!

> *But what if I don't have enough faith?* Jesus honors faith the size of a mustard seed—even faith mixed with doubt!

> *I'm afraid for my loved ones who don't believe much of anything; what will happen to them when they die?* Jesus didn't come into

the world to condemn—but to save. Trust your loved ones to him!

> *I'm so afraid to die; what will the experience of death be like for me?* Jesus promises to never leave you, ever. When it's time, he'll come and hold you, whispering, "I'm here. Have no fear. You're almost home."

When my sister-in-law Paula confidently proclaimed, "For sure, I am not afraid," a few weeks before she died, I'm convinced it wasn't because her faith was greater than yours or mine but because Jesus was with her. The old spiritual gets it right—"When I come to die, give me Jesus."[12] When we're facing mystery, *we long for an assurance only Jesus himself can bring.* An unexplainable assurance that is a gift of Jesus' love and presence . . . in the abiding life.

One Sunday when Caroline was two, she fell and hit her head in her toddler class at church, resulting in a sizeable gash. Carla took the other two girls home while I rushed my wounded sweetheart to the emergency room. I'm not sure Caroline had been in a hospital since her birth, so of course, she was frightened. Everything was new and mysterious, and she clung to me as we were led to a curtained room where a doctor prepared to stitch her up. It crushed me to feel her tremble when they numbed her wound, and to see her flinch when they closed it with needle and thread. I wanted so badly to explain what was happening to my little girl in a way she could understand. I'm sure I tried. But mostly, I held her and whispered over and over, "Daddy's got you. It's going to be alright." My gentle voice called Caroline to trust that I knew what she didn't know. To believe any pain I allowed was for her healing. To surrender to my love—even when she didn't understand.

So it is with us and Jesus. We cling to him when life overwhelms us with unanswerable questions, believing, more importantly, that he will never let go of us. We trust he knows what we long to know but cannot know. We choose to surrender to his love that holds us in the pain, even when we don't understand. My friends, this isn't blind faith but humble trust in our Jesus in the face of mystery. It's the power of his love to secure us in the abiding life.

Then one day, we won't need to trust his love any longer, because we'll be in the presence of our One Great Love. After endless years of trying to see him through the haze and mystery of life's unanswerable questions, we'll finally see him as he's always seen us—face-to-face. On that day, suffering, tears, death, and mystery itself will be no more. The long journey will be over. At last, sons and daughters of God, we'll be . . . home.

Chapter 7

ALONE WITH OUR LOVE

O God, You are my God;

Early will I seek You;

My soul thirsts for You;

My flesh longs for You

In a dry and thirsty land . . .

Because Your lovingkindness is better than life.

PSALM 63:1, 3

Remain in the holy and sweet grace of God. Sweet Jesus, Jesus Love.

ST. CATHERINE OF SIENA

It is not enough to hear of Christ, or read of Christ; but this is the thing
. . . to feel him my root, my life, and my foundation.

ISAAC PENINGTON

Abiding in Jesus' love means learning to be with him alone—where we give him our love and our true selves—and receive him and his love in return.

CARLA AND I HAVE BEEN QUARANTINED together for more than a month because of the pandemic. For the most part, we eat together; take walks together; watch birds together; work in the same room together; watch TV together; laugh and cry together; pray together; and Zoom with pastors, their spouses, and our kids and grandkids . . . together. Late last night, I took Carla in my arms, held her gaze longer than usual, and told her that outside of struggling with my health, this has been one of the best months of my entire life because I have been honored to spend so much time . . . with her. My friend, partner, journey mate—my love. Outside of a few tense moments—after all, we're experiencing an incredibly intense moment in history—our time together has been encouraging, life-giving . . . and most of all, given freely. No coercion or obligation; we want to be together, choose to be together, long to be together—because we're in love.

What if this is exactly how God intends for it to be, longs for it to be, between us and him? What if that sense of duty and burden—along with the baggage of guilt and shame that so often and easily attaches to our "quiet times" with Jesus—doesn't come from God but from hell and is a slice of the enemy's strategy to distance us from God's heart and keep us in bondage? What if the personal disciplines of Bible study and prayer (to name two) were never intended to *primarily* be disciplines but rather welcomed invitations to be together with our One Great Love?

This is the freeing intimacy with Jesus that my young brother Chris unknowingly yearned for when he came to us a few years back as a seminary student, desiring to do his internship at Hope Community Church. He asked if I would be his field instructor. I said yes, and we made plans to sit down and talk about what the internship might look like, both for him and for us.

A couple of weeks later, we met at a local coffee shop, and after a few formalities, Chris opened his sizable internship notebook, slid it across the table toward me, and began to outline what he was doing at Hope—and what he was doing with and for God. Volunteering at Thursday night youth group, helping teach Friday morning Bible study, coleading a neighborhood guys' group on Saturday mornings, serving in children's ministry on Sunday—the list was extensive, impressive . . . and exhausting. But most importantly, Chris told me later, "I wanted to show you my personal devotional plan—how many chapters of the Bible I would read during each session with God, what my prayer time would look like—so that if you ever had a question, I would have an answer!"

I listened attentively, and when Chris was done, I slowly slid his open notebook back across the table and gently closed it. Then I paused, tenderly engaged his eyes, and said, "All this is great, son. But how do *you feel* right now—about God, about yourself, and your life? That's what I want to talk about—not what you're *doing* for God but what's going on inside your heart *with* God."

Chris later shared, "It was like you were speaking a different language. Even though I had a thousand things I needed to share, I couldn't talk to you about my feelings. I was absolutely stuck and shut down."

The more I found out about Chris's story, I wasn't surprised. Growing up in Grand Rapids, Michigan, he never really knew his biological father. There were two stepfathers, and the second felt for a moment like a real dad—but left when Chris was twelve. "I believed in Jesus soon after my second stepfather walked out," Chris recounted, "but I still went on a quest to find that sense of affection, approval, and belonging I longed for from a father." In high school, he tried to fill the emptiness with athletics, booze, women, and violence—ultimately resulting in a drug-possession charge at seventeen and a devastating loss of any chance at a university-football scholarship.

Chris spent his senior year in Georgia, living with a former football coach, his wife, and four children. For the first time in his life, he experienced the healing love of an entire family—and flourished. But healing is a long journey, and Chris needed so much more. When he arrived back in Detroit for his initial semester at Wayne State University, Chris told me he could almost hear Satan say, "Welcome home." For the next two years, he partied hard—again—still trying to fill the love chasm inside his heart. Then one night, deeply moved by memories of his Georgia family's love, Chris had a moment of clarity and on the spot traded forty ouncers, weed, and a deeply flawed relationship with a young woman . . . for Christian authors Watchman Nee, A. W. Tozer, and John Eldredge. In fact, he dove into Christianity with the same passion he brought to the partying scene. The problem is—Chris wasn't really looking for Christianity. His broken heart ached for the healing love of God. Almost prophetically, one evening he wrote in his journal, "Father, come now . . . from one who is Fatherless."

Just a few weeks—and a few more life-altering experiences later—Chris found himself in a church where he finally told God "I'm yours" and laid the partying down for good. "But there was still a huge problem that I really didn't understand at the time," Chris told me a few months back. "I finally got it that booze, drugs, and sex wouldn't give me the affirmation and love I was looking for. But since the day my stepfather left me, I was so terrified of being abandoned again that I was determined not to let men or God get close to me. So, that morning in church, I simply exchanged the partying for a bunch of religious rules. *My new spiritual life became one long list of what I needed to do to prove myself to a God I so desperately wanted to love me.*"

No wonder Chris came to me that morning at the coffee shop so disciplined—and secretly miserable—armed with a rigid, scripted, impressive schedule for connecting with God . . . which didn't connect him with God much at all. Jesus said, "If the Son sets you free, you are truly free" (John 8:36, NLT), but all Chris felt was bondage and exhaustion. Jesus calls us to a lifetime of intimacy—with prayer and Scripture as a place to meet him along the way, to pour out our heart to him and hear his heart in return. "But to me," Chris said, "the Bible and prayer were just a way to receive my marching orders. My plan was to discipline myself to study and pray hard enough that God would approve of me and someday, maybe even love me." An unsustainable, life-stealing plan many of us know all too well.

Chris remembers me sharing with him that morning from the Sermon on the Mount, where over and over, Jesus refers to God as the Father, *our Father*. Then, with *my* fatherly hands wrapped around his, I said, "God is *your* Father, son—and he loves you not for what you do for him but for who you truly are. He's inviting you to let go of performing, of the endless effort to prove yourself—and to let him love you like a beloved son." I encouraged him to go home and pour out his heart to God as a Father who loves him—and to open the Scripture to hear from that same loving Father. Chris told me later that this moment and this truth saved his life—because he finally began to connect with the God whose love has slowly, since that day, *become his life*.

Jesus calls us to abide in his love—a healing life with him that is genuinely, experientially *free*. Yet for some, like Chris, and others who have been shaped by "just do it" Christianity, connecting with Jesus in Scripture or in prayer feels more like bondage, a regimen of shoulds and oughts engulfed in an aura of guilt and shame. A few months back, I received an e-mail from a well-meaning Christian leader who wanted to help me establish "a prayer habit" for the coming year. *Wait*, I thought. *Talking to the One I love needs . . . a habit?* The truth is, even a hint of this kind of dutiful drudgery is exhausting and drains life from any relationship—including our relationship with God—eventually rendering it unsustainable. Who wants to keep "meeting up" with even our closest friend out of obligation, especially if it feels like we never quite pass inspection? Listen carefully: If the spiritual disciplines feel like a burdensome chore, you're on a fast track to spiritual burnout. Soon you'll just go through the motions. Eventually, you won't go there at all.

If we're going to consistently abide in the love of Jesus, it's imperative we embrace this truth: *The spiritual disciplines aren't primarily about discipline.* Alone time with the Lord isn't about striving and duty any more than my alone time with Carla is about gritting my teeth and forcing myself to be with her because it's the right thing to do. "O God . . . I seek you, my soul thirsts for you . . . because your steadfast love is better than life," David cries, with no trace of guilt or duty as motivation (Psalm 63:1, 3, NRSV). Jesus calls us to abide in his love, not sign up for spiritual boot camp.

Still, in any love relationship, *some* discipline is involved because life has a way of distracting us from even our most valued friendships. Sometimes I must discipline myself to say no to demands that pull me in many directions and choose to set aside space for Carla, my family, and close friends. In the same way, Paul talks about disciplining his body like an athlete (1 Corinthians 9:27) as a metaphor of the spiritual life—and I've emphasized that following Jesus is a battle with the powers of darkness, requiring diligence, watchfulness, and spiritual sobriety (Ephesians 6:10-20; 1 Thessalonians 5:6; 1 Peter 4:7). Nevertheless—*the overall ambience of our alone time with Jesus is meant to be passionate love.* This means every spiritual practice, including Bible study and prayer, must be about transformational intimacy, drawing us closer to the heart of our One Great Love. Jesus doesn't demand we spend time with him; he *invites* us to be with him because he loves us.

Take our relationship with the Bible. My first semester in seminary, I always stopped by the campus mailbox right before chapel to hopefully pick up a letter from Carla. We weren't yet engaged but were certainly in love—and her letters were textured, perfumed, and full of encouragement, future dreams, and most of all, words about the deep love we shared. From the mailbox, I walked directly to chapel, and when the speaker began to preach, I would place Carla's open love letter in my open Bible and pretend to listen to the sermon, appropriately nodding my head at the right times and occasionally murmuring a pious amen. But it was all for show. Because I was reading Carla's love letter—over and over—and I literally couldn't get enough!

Years later, I realized that when I removed Carla's love letter from my Bible—I was still reading a love letter. In the Song of Solomon, the young Shulamite bride commands the daughters of Jerusalem, "If you find my beloved . . . tell him I am lovesick" (Song of Solomon, 5:8), referring primarily to her new husband, but also ultimately reflecting our deep love for Jesus Christ.[1] In Psalm 119:97, David gets so excited about connecting with God through his Word, he shouts, "Oh how I love your instructions! I think about them all day long" (NLT). That's where I find myself today with the Bible. I love God's Word, not because I should but because I'm love-sick for my Jesus—and Scripture is one of the main places I find him.

But doesn't the Bible call us to obedience? Of course. Scripture lays out a clear, wise pathway leading to life, warning against the consequences of the only other path available—a foolish avenue of death. Paul's words to Timothy are powerful and timeless: "Every part of Scripture is God-breathed and useful one way or another—showing us truth, exposing our rebellion, correcting our mistakes, training us to live God's way. Through the Word we are put together and shaped up for the tasks God has for us" (2 Timothy 3:14-17, MSG). *But God always calls us to life-giving obedience because of his love for us.* Only his love allows us to trust his words in Scripture—even his most difficult commands and challenges—and consistently obey. In fact, N. T. Wright names God's unconditional, unfailing love "our chief weapon against temptation"![2] Not guilt, fear of failure, or discipline—but God's love.

Those most obedient to the Word of God aren't the most disciplined—but those most deeply connected to his love. My friend Dan[3] served fourteen years in the Michigan prison system—the last eight without a major ticket, which is an absolute miracle in the world of incarceration. When Dan was paroled, he gifted me his prison Bible. The day I opened it, the first thing I noticed were the colors—more verses highlighted than not. But my favorite passage in Dan's Bible is Isaiah 53, where verses 3 through 5 are outlined in blue, underlined in red, and highlighted in yellow: "But he endured the suffering that should have been ours, the pain that we should have borne. . . . We are healed by the punishment he suffered, made whole by the blows he received" (GNT). Just above this prophecy of Messiah's death for us, former violent criminal Dan wrote in bold pink letters, I LOVE YOU JESUS. Dan ravenously consumed and lived the Bible—even behind prison walls—not because he was so disciplined but because he was in love.

But what if we don't feel love from Scripture and in fact feel the opposite—guilt and shame? In high school, my daughter Caroline asked, "Dad, how can I love the Bible when no matter where I look, all I see are commands I haven't obeyed or sins I might have committed?" It's a fair question. What if, to us, the Scripture feels more like an accusatory indictment than a healing, life-giving love letter? And God, the author, seems more like a distant CEO we can never please than a loving Father? What then? My friend Dan's answer is clear: "Take a look at Jesus." That's exactly what Jesus himself said: "Whoever has seen me has seen the Father" (John 14:9, NRSV). Again, Buechner brings this truth home—

If ever there should turn out unbelievably to be a God of love willing to search for men even in the depths of evil and pain, *the face of Jesus is the face we would know him by.*[4]

Strong and courageous, merciful and loving—the face of Jesus has done more to heal my damaged image of the Father and his Word, along with many other deep wounds, than any other single factor. Truthfully, without the face of Jesus, I'm not sure if I would believe in God at all. If you are struggling with the Bible, with the God of the Bible, or with long-term, seeping battle scars . . . *see Jesus.* See him love, comfort, and forgive a wounded young woman in Luke 7 who bathes his feet in her tears of lament. Feel Jesus gently holding and blessing vulnerable children in Mark 10. Immerse yourself in Jesus' crucifixion in Luke 23, where he ignores his own pain and compassionately reaches out to the suffering, unnamed criminal crucified next to him, freely promising eternity *with him* . . . in paradise. Turn to John 21 and drink in the radical love and sheer grace of Jesus' pursuit and emotional healing of his trusted friend, Peter, who denied him in his darkest hour. Ask God to help you see yourself in each struggling, wounded human being Jesus touches—to see Jesus, through them, loving and healing you. Know this: The more you engage Jesus' love in the Word, the more you will experience the Father's healing love in the Word . . . everywhere else.

Which invites the question—how often are those who abide in Jesus' love called to open Scripture? That's like asking how often we should pursue a deep conversation with our best friend or spouse. There's no set schedule or amount of time—love always dictates our answer. But one thing I'm sure of—if our time with God and his Word begins to feel like a burden, we need to pull back and reassess. That same first year of seminary, I was a bellman in a Dallas hotel. One night, I got home from hauling bags around 3:00 a.m., exhausted—but like a good soldier, I got out my Bible with a cup of hot chocolate and collapsed on my bunk for my obligatory "quiet time" with God. What I remember next was bolting out of bed, spewing a mouthful of locker-room language because I had drifted off to sleep and spilled the hot chocolate all over myself, my bed, *and* my Bible. It would be years before I deeply and consistently experienced God's love, but in that moment, it was as if God said, "It's not about duty or guilt, son. Let go." So early that morning, covered in chocolate stickiness, I promised myself I would never again pick up the Scripture . . . unless it was from my heart. And I've kept that promise. Listen carefully—if reading and studying the Scripture feels like duty or about gaining God's approval, lay the book down for a while. When you start to miss him, you'll pick up your Bible again. Only this time, you'll be free.

There are other "disciplines" we could talk about—each of which, like Bible study, are simply gracious invitations to be with the God who loves us. But for the rest of this chapter, I want to focus on the privilege of prayer. *Because more than any other spiritual practice, prayer is the soul of the abiding life*—much like authentic sharing of the heart is at the very center of any vibrant, intimate relationship. Prayer is a privilege because we're talking to God himself—but as we've already said, it's a mystery because who can figure out how it works?

At the end of my years as lead pastor, I decided to preach an extended, open-ended series on prayer—because after decades of following Jesus, I still struggled to understand what it meant to pray effectively. After pouring over and teaching more than twenty-five biblical passages on prayer, I reached a conclusion: If we're looking for a tightly packaged "prayer formula"—especially a detailed blueprint on how to get our prayers answered—we won't find one in Scripture. That is *not* to say there are no prayer signposts. "Though you offer many prayers, I will not listen," God says to rebellious, hypocritical Israel in the eighth century, "for your hands are covered with the blood of innocent victims" (Isaiah 1:15, NLT). God isn't saying, "Be perfect or don't pray," but rather, "I will not be used. Come to me with sincerity of heart and life, or don't waste your breath." In the New Testament, James names the prophet Elijah as someone who "prayed hard" and God answered, *not* to bait us into generating passion so our prayers will be heard—but to encourage us to come to him with deep, authentic need (James 5:16-18, MSG). There are many other markers, but no formula, because for God, prayer is too intimate and profoundly personal to be about spiritual recipes and equations.

In fact, what I discovered was what I suspected all along: Prayer isn't primarily about answers at all, but, like reading the Bible, about our *passionate longing to connect with our One Great Love*. George McDonald asks,

What if the main object in God's idea of prayer be the supplying of our great, our endless need—the need of himself?[5]

Prayer was never meant to be primarily about getting something from God—or even about God meeting our legitimate needs—*but about us simply being with him*. In Matthew, Jesus acknowledges his listeners' desperate need for food and clothing, but instead of offering a "foolproof prayer formula," remarkably says, "Your heavenly Father already knows your needs. Seek the Kingdom of God above all else . . . and he will give you everything you need" (Matthew 6:32-33, NLT). In other words, "Don't obsess about answers. Focus on your relationship with your Father—and trust that he's taking care of everything." In the same way, David consistently cries, "O LORD, do not be far from Me," longing first and foremost for God's nearness (Psalm 22:19). Likewise, Paul promises peace in anxiety, not because we're sure to receive every desired answer to every prayer but because we surrender our worry to a Lord who "is near" (Philippians 4:5, NRSV). Of course we have needs—but what if our greatest need is connecting with him?

This *doesn't* mean we can't also ask him for what we need. Prayers for wisdom (James 1:5-8), forgiveness (Matthew 6:12; 1 John 1:5-10), and guidance (Psalm 31:1-3; 48:14) are as common as breathing in the abiding life. In fact, Jesus commands, "Ask, and it will be given to you" (Luke 11:9). Yet, even when asking the Father to meet our needs, Jesus calls us to focus *not* on answers, but on trusting the relationship:

> Don't bargain with God. Be direct. Ask for what you need.
> This is not a cat-and-mouse, hide-and-seek game we're in.
> If your little boy asks for a serving of fish, do you scare him
> with a live snake on his plate? If your little girl asks for an
> egg, do you trick her with a spider? As bad as you are, you
> wouldn't think of such a thing. . . . And don't you think *the
> Father who conceived you in love* will give the Holy Spirit
> when you ask him?
>
> LUKE 11:10-13, MSG, EMPHASIS ADDED

Carla is on the phone—right now—trying to get me an appointment with a specialist for the undiagnosed illness I've battled for several weeks. A moment ago, I stopped writing, bowed my head, and whispered, "Father, please . . ." That's all. No formula. I didn't even finish the prayer out loud. He knows my heart, what I need. He knows we're anxious and would love some answers. So I'm unashamedly asking him for answers. In fact, I'm asking him to heal me. But that's not the main reason I prayed a moment ago. I prayed because I'm desperate to talk with my heavenly Father. To know he's listening, that he is with me. I prayed in order to abide in the protective, strengthening love of the One who "conceived me in love."

Look, I know some of you are profoundly discouraged about prayer right now—even wondering if God is listening at all. I sat with a close friend a few months ago as she sobbed, "God, where are you? Why have you left me?" Many of us are simply burned out from obsessing about how to "pray right," always scrambling to get God's attention, imagining him scrutinizing every motive, every prayerful syllable, all while carrying crushing false guilt about some supposed, overlooked prayer protocol that "caused" him to say no to the cry of our heart. I've lived that performance-laden bondage—it's the loneliest kind of hell on earth. But what if prayer is simply "the sound made by our deepest aloneness"?[6] What if prayer isn't a religious prison—but you and me *freely reaching out from desperate isolation to the God who loves us and longs to be with us?* Imagine climbing onto your heavenly Father's lap, pouring out your heart as he holds you in his everlasting arms. Picture Jesus right beside you as you share every joy, every sorrow, while he listens with deep compassion and attentive love.

This way of looking at prayer changes *everything*—first, because it means we can tell God *everything*. We can pray with a fresh, liberating honesty that's a by-product of his unconditional love. Many relationships warn, "Tell me what I want to hear, or I will reject you." In these friendships, intimacy is hindered by what we hide. But our God eagerly beckons: *Share everything with me because I love you—the real you. And I will never leave you—ever* (Hebrews 13:5). Imagine never hiding anything from God again. Never pretending, never looking away in shame, but safely gazing into his eyes and allowing him to love and receive every piece of us—even thoughts, feelings, and actions that need deep healing and forgiveness. Imagine finally *experiencing* the rumored, longed-for closeness with God we were convinced was only for the other guy but now realize is available to any of his sons and daughters—if we're willing to trust his love enough to take off our masks.

Radical vulnerability—which is everywhere in Scripture—is the *only* pathway to the intimacy with God we long for. The Psalms are full of David's raw, unfiltered prayers as he pours out every thought and emotion—joy, sorrow, lament, praise, struggle, and sin (even the sins of adultery and premeditated murder)—to the God who is his refuge (Psalm 51; 62:8). In one of my favorite New Testament images, a compassionate Jesus beckons us to come to him boldly because he feels with us in all our weaknesses (Hebrews 4:14-16). Paul instructs us to tell God everything (Philippians 4:6), and Peter invites us to "give all your worries and cares to God, for he cares about you" (1 Peter 5:7, NLT). Dear friend, can you feel the freedom? Abiding in Jesus' love means we can send our exhausting, performance-based "pretend prayers" back to hell—and embrace the breathtaking abandon of telling Jesus what is really going on. All the time. All the way home.

When we begin to talk to God honestly, the truth shatters every other prayer shackle in our lives. As a kid, I remember feeling hammered by Paul's command, "Pray all the time" (1 Thessalonians 5:16-18 MSG). I simply didn't want to pray that much—but even if I did, I'd never be holy enough to pull it off. But once I discovered God loved me, loved being with me—and it was safe to tell him everything—I began to talk to him all day. All night. Literally, "all the time." I've caught drivers staring at me at a stoplight like I'm a crazy person because they see me in an otherwise empty car, talking to no one. Of course, I'm talking to him.

When my daughter Andrea was two, she would run to the window when I pulled into the driveway, shouting excitedly in her little girl voice, "Daddy's home!" She couldn't wait for me to walk in the door so we could wrestle, play hide-and-seek, read books, and chat about the day because along with Carla, I was her whole world. In the same way, I have a running conversation with Jesus—not because I'm disciplined or religious, but because I love him and there's never a moment I don't miss him, need him, and need to talk to him about . . . everything. I pray all the time because Jesus is my world. I tell him I love him; or thank you very much; or please take care of Carla, my girls, and their families; or forgive me—I did that thing again; or I'm afraid, angry, or excited. I talk to him about the Chicago Cubs, my closest friends, pastors and their families, dreams, disappointments, my favorite beer, and the guy who just cut me off in traffic. I laugh with him, but I also lift my broken heart, along with the pain and injustice I see around me and around the world. Sometimes, like David, I shout, "Where are you?" begging him to show up and do his job. It's a moment-by-moment, radically vulnerable conversation through life with the One who is my world . . . my One Great Love.

Look, there's nothing wrong with scheduling specific prayer times—Jesus sometimes did (Mark 6:46; Luke 6:12). On one of his prayer retreats, Jesus talked to God all night—not because he was disciplined but because, just like us, he needed to be with his Father. Liturgical prayers are also cool if that's your thing. Jesus taught us his prayer, and every line is saturated with deep relationship (Matthew 6:9-15). But here's the point: When you start talking to the Father with unvarnished, gut-level honesty, your trying-hard-to-pray days are over. Prayer won't be about discipline any longer, but a simple reaching out from your seeming aloneness to the One who loves you and the One you love, the God you can't stand to be away from . . . even for a moment. The Jesus who is your whole world.

And then, one day, catalyzed by the same radical honesty—power shows up. In the mid-1990s, I traveled with some brothers to Uganda to share Jesus and teach the game of baseball. We stayed in the capital city of Kampala, still recovering from Idi Amin's reign of terror fifteen years earlier. Infrastructure was scant (one stoplight for a million people), poverty rampant, and medical care in short supply. But the Ugandan people were profoundly gracious and truly kind, and they possessed a resilient, courageous faith.

One evening, I was called to a home to pray for a Ugandan brother who was ill with a frightening, unknown fever. I'm ashamed that at first, I didn't want to go—because I was afraid. What if my prayer for healing didn't work? Back home, I had prayed for many extremely sick people—but always with a backup plan. If my prayers fell short, the best medical care in the world stood ready to pick up where God left off. But that day in Uganda, I knew there was no backup plan for this dear, struggling brother—or for me, if I happened to get sick from laying my hands on him in Jesus' name.

That evening, I walked into a dimly lit room in a Kampala neighborhood, where I was affectionately greeted by several Ugandan brothers and sisters and introduced to the young man looking for healing. I don't remember his name, but I'll never forget his face and the desperate, hopeful way he looked into my eyes. We sat together for a few moments and then, after asking permission, I gently placed my inadequate, trembling hands on his head and began to talk to God, first silently—and vulnerably.

"Father, You know I believe in you . . . but I'm so afraid. Either you're here—now—with your love and power, or I've got nothing. Please, help me do battle with the powers of darkness for the life of your wounded son, through Jesus Christ our Lord." Then I opened my mouth *and prayed like I had never, ever prayed before.*

It's difficult to explain. I wasn't trying to pray powerfully. I didn't pray louder or longer. But I prayed with conviction, faith, and power that poured from my heart to God's heart in a way I had never previously experienced. It was as if desperate honesty with God about the intensity of the struggle with hell for the young brother's life, in the face of my feelings of fear and inadequacy, transported me to a place intended to be the launch site for all our prayers. This I know: Every call to prayer in the Bible is written to an audience that possessed no backup plan. When they prayed, they cried out to God with *fierce honesty* about their overwhelming need, raw fear, and desperate longing to be rescued. To be loved. To be healed. To live with hope. To defeat the darkness. They prayed honestly—about everything—with conviction, faith, and power . . . because they had nowhere else to go. Perhaps if we were honest about the flimsy nature of our backup plans and more vulnerable about how desperately we need him— perhaps we, too, would pray with more power. Not because we're trying hard. But because praying the radical truth about life takes us there.

And just in case you're wondering—I heard a few weeks later that after our prayer time, the Ugandan brother's fever lifted. Maybe it went away on its own. Maybe Jesus healed him. You know what I believe.

Let me close with a picture. When my girls were small and got hurt or scared, they would run to me, fly into my arms, lay their head on my chest, and sob out their pain. Occasionally, I would share words—but often, I would simply hold them so they could feel my strong love. After some time, they invariably pushed away and, with new energy, sprinted back to their lives. What happened to their cares? Why, they left them on the strong, loving chest of their father. Mysteriously, their fear, sadness, and weakness were exchanged for their daddy's healing love, comfort, and strength. And this intimate heart exchange between father and daughter set them free.

Isaiah prophesied Messiah coming to give God's people "beauty *for* ashes, the oil of joy *for* mourning, the garment of praise *for* the spirit of heaviness"—an exchange that frees all to be "trees of righteousness . . . that He [the Lord] may be glorified" (Isaiah 61:3, emphasis added). What if this holy exchange is prayer? What if it is studying his Word? What if it is a picture of all the spiritual disciplines? Sons and daughters running to our Father because we love him and long to offer him everything in our heart—pain, praise, and all that is in between. And, as we run to him, we receive from him exactly what we need to live for his glory . . . every moment, every day, all the way home. You know what I call that? Freedom.

This is what it means to get alone with your One Great Love: Say good night to duty and shame and good morning to passion and longing. Leave behind the misery and burden of obligation and welcome the grace of invitation. Lay down a lifetime of performance and embrace Jesus' unconditional love—for you—in the freedom of the abiding life.

Chapter 8

HEALING LOVE IN JESUS' COMMUNITY

Where two or three are gathered together in My name,
I am there in the midst of them.

MATTHEW 18:20

How inexhaustible are the riches that open up for those who . . . are
privileged to live in the daily fellowship of life with other Christians!

DIETRICH BONHOEFFER

The primary building blocks for the corporate temple of God . . . are
covenantal relationships in which believers know one another profoundly,
love one another deeply, and care for one another unconditionally. Only
in this way do we grow in Christ.

GREG BOYD

**Abiding in Jesus' love is learning to receive the
healing love offered to us by the brothers and
sisters of Jesus himself.**

WHEN I WAS A LITTLE BOY, my grandmother Lela was my favorite
grown-up. When I was with her, I felt emotionally safe. I loved it
when our family made the trek to Ohio to stay with her for a few
days. Most of the time when we visited, my grandma had several
people staying with her who needed to feel safe like me. Her brother,
my great-uncle Irion, was one of them. He was single and, as far as
I could tell, didn't have many friends; even his other brothers and
sisters didn't have much to do with him. When he wasn't at work, he

stayed in his room, coming out only for meals. He didn't say much and didn't smile much, but he was always nice to me.

Eventually Irion died and I grew up. A few years ago, I stumbled on my uncle's set of century-old, high-school Eclectic English Classics— including works by Shakespeare, Eliot, Tennyson, and Irving, most of which I had never read. Excited, I dove in, beginning with Sir Walter Scott's *Ivanhoe*. As I read late one night, I was astounded by what I found on page 372—not from Scott's pen but from my then-seventeen-year-old uncle's broken heart. In the yellowed upper margin, penciled in and around the chapter heading, he'd scrawled these words:

Irion V. Jacob—many days alone along life's pathway.

And there he was—my real uncle Irion. Maybe not so reclusive after all. Or even all that quiet or strange. But simply, alone. Though not yet twenty years old—for many days, alone.

In that moment, I wanted so badly to go back in time and tell him that he was important to me. I wanted him to know I loved him, that it must have been so tough to feel so alone, that he was never meant to be alone. And, as I stared at page 372 for a while longer, I realized something else: in his aloneness, my uncle represents us all.

A few years ago, I attended a conference where psychiatrist Dr. Curt Thompson noted that we all take an anxious, grief-filled journey down the birth canal, and each of us, without exception, enters the world alone. Immediately we're so naturally uncomfortable with our aloneness that our first newborn breath is a cry of longing to be connected—we desperately start "looking for someone looking for us . . . with delight." Dr. Thompson reflected, "I'm fifty-six years old—and today, I still long for the same thing."[1]

Because here's the deal: Though we're all born into the cosmic aloneness of a broken world, each of us is created in the likeness of a God who is Father, Son, and Spirit, and who has lived in face-to-face relationship with himself for all eternity. His very essence is intimate relationship. No matter who we are, whatever our background, circumstances, or personality type, "many days alone along life's pathway" is not our destiny. We begin life in aloneness—but it simply isn't in our nature to continue to do life alone.

God said as much to Adam: "It's not good for the Man to be alone; I'll make him . . . a companion" (Genesis 2:18-20, MSG). Don't miss the irony—at the very moment God spoke these words, not only was Adam *not* alone but his exclusive, intimate companion was God himself! With God, Adam was never bored, worried, or afraid. He never wanted for anything. Yet, relationally, something was still missing. According to God, Adam was still, in a very real sense . . . alone.

God's answer to Adam's aloneness? To create a being "who is just right for him," a woman named Eve, to be his partner (Genesis 2:18, NLT), so that neither of them would walk alone. Of course, there's much here about marriage, but there's also a broader application: *Our desperate longing for "someone looking for us . . . with delight" isn't only about our need to connect personally with God—but about our deep need to connect with one another.* It's not that God wasn't enough for Adam or Eve, or that he isn't enough for us. But God created us to connect not only with him directly but also through relationship with others in whom he lives. Even Jesus himself—possessing a vibrant, powerful relationship with the Father—called twelve men and several women to walk closely with him on his earthly journey. And in his darkest hour, as he moved toward Gethsemane to pour out his heart to his Father one last time, Jesus also wanted—needed—Peter, James, and John by his side.

Abiding in Jesus' love is more than personal Bible study, personal prayer, personal journaling, and personal consumption of sermons, podcasts, and worship music. As sweet, powerful, and necessary as our personal time with Jesus is, it's not enough to sustain us on the journey. Not enough to heal us and make us whole. We need the community of Jesus. We need the people in whom Jesus dwells. We need a lifetime of intimate, authentic connection with other sons and daughters of God. To abide, we don't just need Christ—we desperately need the body of Christ.

For some of us, this might be good news. Western Christianity puts a great deal of unwarranted pressure on our personal connection with God. We're taught to get alone with him, to hear his voice and feel his love—fair enough—but when it doesn't work out for us like we think it should, we panic and think, *Maybe he doesn't love me* or *I'm not doing it right*, resulting in guilt, shame, and discouragement. Let me be clear: I'm *not* saying God doesn't speak to us, "touch" us, or begin to heal us when we're alone with him—because I think he can and does. But what if the lens of Western individualism has caused us to ignore—or at least relegate to second-tier status—the biblical call to *experience the love and healing presence of Jesus in and through his community*? What if we've become so addicted to our individual spiritual rhythms—getting alone with God in the desert or the coffee shop—that we take less seriously Jesus' words, "When two or three of you are together because of me, you can be sure that *I'll be there*" (Matthew 18:18-20, MSG, emphasis added)? Or Paul's defining discourse to the Corinthian church on how we simply *cannot* make it without one another?

Each of us is now a part of [Christ's] resurrection body. . . .
     The way God designed our bodies is a model for understanding our lives together . . . *every part dependent on every other part.* . . . If one part hurts, every other part is involved in the hurt, and in the healing. . . .

You are Christ's body—that's who you are! *You must never forget.*

I CORINTHIANS 12:12-13, 25-31, MSG, EMPHASIS ADDED

Our profound need for one another isn't just theology—it's human biology. "The brain can do a lot," Dr. Thompson went on to say at the conference I referenced earlier, "but it doesn't function well alone. Our brains must have connection to flourish." Then he said something I'll never forget: "After years of research and clinical practice, I've come to believe everything we ask for and long for in the world is proxy for relationship. Our suffering is mostly about . . . *isolation*."[2]

Listen—I know some of us are really struggling to abide in the love of Jesus. Right now. Maybe for a long while. Could this truth be a colossal piece of what we've been missing? That intimate connection with other brothers and sisters in the body of Christ isn't arbitrary or optional but like breathing—absolutely necessary for life in our relationship with Jesus? Could it be urgently, vitally true that, as pastor and songwriter Hezekiah Walker said, "I need you, you need me . . . / . . . to survive"?[3]

Take my last few months. I live in deep community. My wife, Carla, is not only my best friend but my serious sister in Christ. The girl knows me and knows Jesus, and we walk in his love *together*. I also have three pastor friends who are like brothers—Bill, Carlton, and Ed—and we've laughed, cried, cussed, prayed, preached, stumbled, and soared our way through the last thirty-five years of life with Jesus Christ *together*. Then, out of nowhere, the pandemic. Social distancing. Isolation. And after only eight weeks, my brokenness—and desperate need for even deeper community—was exposed.

I'm a little anxious about sharing what comes next because vulnerability is a bit frightening. If I get too honest, I might be misunderstood and maybe even rejected. But the truth is, when I got seriously sick during the lockdown and my symptoms were relentless and my three daughters were thirteen hundred miles away and the medical system was overrun and partially shut down, and we struggled to get a diagnosis or to see a doctor face-to-face—I got afraid. Then angry. Then sad. Then depressed. My faith wavered. I wondered and doubted. About heaven. About prayer. About human suffering. I found myself grieving stories of believers and nonbelievers alike—around me, around the world—who were hurting, struggling, crying out. Years of studying the Bible and church history, thousands of sermons preached, and hundreds of God books read—all of it meant little. I began to shut down. I didn't want to talk to anyone. I avoided my daughters' texts and calls and didn't share my deepest reality with the three brothers I'd walked with for decades. I talked to God, but he was silent. I slowly slid into despair. Carla was the only one who knew. She saw me drifting away—but wasn't sure what to do.

Then, as if out of nowhere, the body of Christ showed up. Brothers and sisters outside the intimate crew I did life with—members of Jesus' community who knew little about my present darkness— mysteriously moved toward me, in love. Jeff and Meredith, a young couple we'd known somewhat casually for years, brought us dinner and ice cream—more than once—and one particularly anxious night, brought Jesus to my brokenness in their FaceTime pleas to God on my behalf. They had no answers. They didn't try to fix me. They simply prayed with deep compassion *for me*, a broken servant of Christ. I wept. And for the first time in a while, I felt healing peace.

Soon, others reached out. Carla's friend Luanna, whom I barely know. Audrey, a thirty-year friend who sensed I was hiding. Caitlyn, a writing colleague who reminds me so much of my daughters, and

Peter, a gifted young pastor I often call son. All pursued me, the one who so often pursues . . . and prayed for me, the one always more comfortable doing the praying. Without prompting, each asked for my healing—unaware that I hadn't often been able to ask for healing myself. And slowly, powerfully, though I still battled physical symptoms, these healing prayers began to put my fragile faith . . . and me . . . back together again.

So many others texted or called—Abel and Marie, William, Kevin, Rick, Chuck, Lori, Doug, and more—each with a unique, different kind of "healing gift" and story of how they felt moved by Jesus to connect. And then, one afternoon, Pam—for years a pastor and partner at Hope Community—called to check in. Through tears, I responded more vulnerably than I had in weeks: "Pam, I feel . . . lost." Tenderly, she asked, "Kevin, in your weakness, can you let Jesus be your strength? He leaves the ninety-nine and always pursues the lost one. Will you let him come and rescue you?" That's all. And I was undone. *It was as if Jesus Christ himself was loving me through Pam's words.* Because he was. He exposed my pride, which had isolated and hidden the real me behind the false, macho image of the strong one, the one many call leader, pastor, papa. In two short months, I had drifted from life-giving community . . . to the isolation and suffering of "many days alone along life's pathway." Pastor Pam's loving care called out areas in my spirit that needed repentance, healing, and freedom. And, *along with all the others*, helped me find my way home. "You are Christ's body," Paul said. "You must never forget."

Listen, the healing my brokenness longed for couldn't be found simply in a sermon or a song or, in this case, even in my time alone with the Jesus I love. In each of the three categories of battle wounds in this life—damaged emotions, false beliefs, and trauma—I was bleeding out. Fear, depression, despair. *There is no heaven, God doesn't hear our prayers, I'm going to die during the pandemic and never see my daughters again.* And daily echoes of our long, traumatic journey through Carla's cancer.

"Just do it" Christianity says, "Pray and study the Bible harder. Listen to a podcast. Renew your mind. Repent. Be thankful." None are wrong in proper context. But in that moment, my aloneness didn't need a shaming, spiritual to-do list—I needed the healing of Jesus Christ, in and through the presence of other sons and daughters of God. "When two or three of you are together," Jesus promised, "you can be sure that *I'll be there.*"

Some of you might ask, "How exactly does this work?" But spiritual power can't be reduced to scientific explanation. No doubt this healing is mysterious, Kingdom-of-God-on-earth stuff. But I guarantee it's real. And the healing agent is *the powerful love of Jesus Christ.* This is why Peter—a man who needed much healing himself— trumpeted to the early church, "Above all, maintain constant love for one another, for love covers a multitude of sins" (1 Peter 4:8, NRSV). This bold word at least means that God's love is meant to generate an attitude of mercy in our hearts toward fellow sinners. But it also points to another mind-blowing reality: *Sin's hellish, deadly impact on our lives cannot survive an onslaught of the love of God's Son.* When we pour out the love of Jesus Christ on one another—even awkwardly, clumsily, humanly—hell retreats. Every time. Listen: Spiritual healing isn't about our totally pure motives, perfectly timed Bible verses, magnitude of service, or profound answers. In fact, the deepest questions have no answers. Every act of love is imperfect because we're imperfect. But even still—the love that led Jesus to the Cross and raised him from the dead always, always prevails.

The church of Jesus Christ is meant to be *the sacred community* where every sin-generated wound can be touched by the love of the

Healer—through the love of his brothers and sisters. But this healing won't take place if we attend church services like we attend movies or sporting events. Sitting for an hour or two in a building, staring at a stage, doesn't create much space for the kind of work Jesus wants to do deep in our souls. Remember, each of us has been attacked and wounded by the "roaring lion, prowling around seeking whom he may devour" (1 Peter 5:8, author's paraphrase).[4] He has injured us emotionally, drilled his poisonous lies into our psyche, and battered us with traumatic events and circumstances. We don't need a spiritual coach. We need a Deliverer.

So, how do we connect with one another in a way that allows the love of Jesus to heal us? First, we've got to let go of our "Sunday is enough" mentality. In the ancient world, the church not only gathered formally once a week but informally every day (Acts 2:46). These brothers and sisters of Jesus were true family, interdependent, connected by the Holy Spirit (1 Corinthians 12:13). We can't expect ancient-church healing if we stay locked in to twenty-first-century "see you next week," shallow church protocol.

Then, speaking of Sundays, we must abandon our addiction to stimulating worship services—especially to the sermon and the song. Don't misunderstand—"the apostles' teaching" and "psalms and hymns and spiritual songs" were an important *part* of early-church gatherings for worship. Jesus was—and still is—present to his followers in and through both (Acts 2:42; Colossians 3:16). But the key word is *part*. No matter how powerful the teaching or how heartfelt the music, these things were never meant to be everything. The Lord's Table; deep and personal prayer; intimate, face-to-face fellowship— all of that and more were also part of weekly worship that healed broken lives (Acts 2:42). But if we continue to make even the best preaching and the most Christ-honoring music "everything"—often

hopping from church to church to find just what our palates are looking for—we will find ourselves rich in information and experience
but utterly lacking in healing community.

But, most crucially—and I cannot say this strongly enough—
when the ancient church came together, whether formally for worship or informally in daily life, *it was never about the professional leader*
but about every believer offering something, in the love of Jesus, to
and for one another.[5] Paul is crystal clear on this point:

> When you gather for worship, *each one of you* be prepared
> with something that will be useful for all: Sing a hymn,
> teach a lesson, tell a story, lead a prayer, provide an insight
> . . . *and you all learn from each other.*
>
> I CORINTHIANS 14:26-33, MSG, EMPHASIS ADDED

Peter echoes the same truth in the context of everyday living:
"God has given *each of you* a gift from his great variety of spiritual
gifts. Use them well to serve one another" (1 Peter 4:10, NLT, emphasis added). This is the bottom line: To heal, *we must create space in
our worship and in our everyday lives to touch and be touched by one
another.* Paul is clear, "If one part hurts, *every other part is involved in
the hurt, and in the healing.*" There is no other way.

The early church struggled with all the same pain, sin, and trauma
that we do—plus persecution and widespread poverty—without
therapists, social workers, support groups, food banks, adequate
medical care, Christian books, or formally trained clergy. The New
Testament documents weren't yet completed, let alone compiled. In
fact, the average believer wouldn't have a personal copy of the entire
Bible for another fourteen hundred years. And yet the ancient body
of Christ didn't just survive but flourished as a healing community.

When second-century apologist Aristides wrote Roman Emperor Hadrian, comparing Christianity with other ancient religions, he boasted, "But the Christians, O King . . . they love one another."[6] He described a community that consistently knelt in radical, costly, face-to-face, merciful service to one another—receiving orphans and widows, elevating slaves to the status of family, burying those who died alone, and starving themselves to feed others during famine. In Jesus Christ and through his love, the powerless possessed a power not of this world, able to heal the wounds of hell.

Brothers and sisters—that same healing is still available today.

My friend Samson[7] was a profoundly abused little boy, and in 2005, he came to us at Hope Community Church a strong but extremely angry young man. The love of Hope's believers brought Samson to Jesus—but he landed in federal prison anyway, where today he's still following Jesus as he walks down his time. A year into Carla's battle with cancer, Samson sent her a handwritten prayer via prison mail:

Dear Lord

I come to you as a broken man for my friend Carla who have a upcoming cancer scan. I pray deep from my heart that nothing shows up their and it's gone for good. If I can ask for anything . . . take me instead of her . . . I been through so much already in my life I willing to go through the pain and scare for Carla. I willing to give my life up to save hers like Jesus did for me on the cross. If I can remove my name out of the book of life for someone Carla would be one of the persons I can do this for— for my lord and savior, in all things, Jesus Christ. Amen.

Samson

Carla is twenty years older than Samson. She was raised in small-town Indiana; Samson grew up deep in urban Detroit. Samson is African American; Carla is Caucasian. Samson's doing a long stint in prison; Carla's a retired teacher. But here's the power—Samson and Carla are brother and sister in Christ, two people who know the love of Christ and who love each other in Christ. Before Samson went to prison, they didn't just sit in the same sanctuary, listen to the same Bible lectures, or wave to each other in the same parking lot. *They took the time to know each other.* They shared jokes—they both love to laugh—and shared meals. They had a relationship. When Samson went to prison, he didn't forget. Carla told me, "In all my years as a pastor's wife—no one has ever said anything to me like Samson said in his letter. In fact, I've been so hurt by church—but this brother is willing to give his life for me? God used the University of Michigan medical team to heal my cancer physically, but he used the love of Jesus in Samson to help heal deep wounds in my spirit."

In other words, Carla couldn't make it without Samson and the Jesus who dwells in Samson. If you don't have these kinds of relationships in the body of Jesus Christ, you're struggling. Or coasting. Or hiding. Or trying to hang on through sheer will. But you're not healing. And you're not free.

Connection that heals is honest, vulnerable, raw, and real. The last verse in Genesis 2—right before the Fall—describes God's design for life-giving relationships: "And the man and his wife were both naked, and were not ashamed" (Genesis 2:25, NRSV). This doesn't just mean physical vulnerability but emotional and spiritual vulnerability too. Life as God intended is you and me, living face-to-face—nothing hidden, nothing to fear—sharing a life-giving intimacy that reflects the eternal communion of Father, Son, and Spirit. But, as we see a few verses later in Genesis, Adam and Eve sinned, and shame and relational fear entered the world. They hid—from themselves, one another, and God. And when they hid, they began to die. We've been hiding and dying ever since.

Paul is crystal clear about our first nonnegotiable step toward community that heals: "No more lies, no more pretense. *Tell your neighbor the truth.* In Christ's body we're all connected to each other, after all" (Ephesians 4:25, MSG, emphasis added). Truth is the first step. Truth about who we really are and what's really going on. Paul is calling us back, in Jesus, to Genesis 2:25—to the joy and freedom of transparent relationship.

Don't misunderstand—casual relationships in the body of Christ are necessary and fun, and of course, it's impossible and even inappropriate to tell everyone everything. But most of us are already all-too-comfortable with purposely shallow friendships. What we struggle with is *radical, pre-Fall Eden authenticity*—a relational vulnerability that releases the healing power of the love of Jesus Christ.

This absolute honesty is so crucial to the healing process. Several years ago, I gathered a group of brothers committed to walking together in vulnerability, and Damon was the first young man I asked to join. He was incredibly gifted—a degree in theater, creative, sensitive, avid reader, skilled writer, loyal friend. But like the rest of us, Damon was deeply wounded—to start with, a father who left him as a child, never took a real interest in him, yet preached at a church every Sunday, noticeably lapping up the praise he loved more than spending time with his son. Also like the rest of us, Damon was stuck in some sinful behavior patterns he couldn't shake, places in his soul that needed healing. But Damon was a master at hiding behind his entertaining sense of humor. And as he hid, he was held captive. Knowing that broke my heart. I love him and knew that deep inside, behind his smiling mask, he was a wounded son of God.

Then one night, everything changed. During group, Damon shared a heart-wrenching personal story, but concluded it in typical fashion—with a hilarious one-liner that deflected any attempt to probe further. Something inside me—maybe the Holy Spirit—said, "Now's the time." After the laughter died down, I leaned forward from my corner chair and asked, "Why is it, son, that the story you just told made me cry . . . but you're laughing, as if it's all a joke? We love you. You're safe here. You don't need to hide anymore."

A sacred quiet filled the room. We all realized that our brother had come to a critical juncture—stay hidden and die, or get honest and begin a healing journey to freedom. Damon could have cracked another joke, told me to back off, or walked out the door—but instead, he courageously decided to get honest. He told us he had been running from his childhood pain for a while, that it had cost him—and that he didn't want to live that way anymore. It was a turning point. Before that moment, Damon lived in bondage to his wounds. But that night, he *told the truth*, and with the love of brothers in Christ surrounding him, the truth began to set him free. Fifteen years later, he's courageously, skillfully, lovingly helping others get free as well.

You might say, "Good for Damon, but I don't want anyone knowing my business. It's between me and God." But this hesitation isn't really about privacy, is it? It's about your fear of being exposed, of being hurt. Believe me, I understand. My honesty has at times been viciously betrayed over the years—and if you live vulnerably, you might get hurt too. *But living the truth has also saved my life.* In truth, I have been surrounded by life-giving brothers and sisters who haven't judged, tried to fix, or walked away, but who helped me heal by loving me well. So shall it be for you—if you drop your mask. Leave it on, and I don't care who you are and how well you *think* you're doing—in reality, you're dying already. And while you stay stuck in hell's mess, the broken world around you stays stuck too.

A few years back, I asked my friend John why I hadn't seen him on Sundays for a while. He said, "Sorry, Pastor, but church isn't really doing much for me right now."

I asked him, "What if it isn't about you? What if, every time we gather, there's someone who doesn't really need my sermon . . . but needs what *you* bring to the table as a transparent son of God?"

John called me excitedly the following Sunday afternoon. "Pastor, you'll never guess what happened. I came into church, sat down next to this white guy I didn't know—and during the prayer time he said, 'I'm an alcoholic, and I'm trying to live in recovery. Lately, it's been really hard.' I told him, 'I feel you because I spent thirty years in the streets—so you're not alone.' Then we prayed together, and it was so good . . . for both of us." I have no idea what I preached on that morning, but this I know—two struggling sons of God came to church that day . . . and were touched by the healing Jesus.

Finally, and maybe most crucially for today's left-brain-dominated, content-oriented, word-saturated Western church: Words alone aren't enough to heal us. *To transform us into the image of Christ, the love of Jesus Christ must be embodied.*

Look, it would be convenient if every Sunday, struggling sons and daughters of God could line up, share their pain, and hear a "word" from a fellow believer that brings instant freedom. A brother or sister might vulnerably share, "I know the Bible *says* God loves the world . . . but I don't think he could love someone . . . like me." Then we could compassionately reply, "Wow, so sorry. But you're wrong. He really does love you. The Scripture doesn't lie. Next in line, please."

But merely saying words doesn't create healing. God himself, the most powerful wordsmith in the universe, came to earth to embody his love—"The Word became flesh and dwelt among us" (John 1:14)—so we could not only read and hear but see, feel, and experience the glory and power of God's love and truth. When we put flesh on the love of God, its power is unleashed.

One night in men's group, our leader Bryan shared that his five-year-old son recently said, "Dad, sometimes I don't think you like me very much." Bryan was floored. He intentionally told Eli multiple times a day that he loved him. Bryan had grown up without a dad, and he purposed to give his own son a different life. But instead of reacting, he thought more about Eli's words and realized, "I'm generally busy when Eli's around and wants to play. I'm always saying, 'Just a minute, son' or trying to do two or three things at once when we're together."

So Bryan began to schedule times—at least once a week—for just Eli and him. Chuck E. Cheese, the park, a movie, taking a walk. "No distractions," Bryan explained to us. "Just me and my son." Bryan didn't stop telling Eli that he loved him. He simply embodied his loving words with the gift of time. Focused attention. Presence. It wasn't long before everything changed. Not only did Eli stop saying, "Dad, I don't think you like me very much," but at school, Eli went from struggling to flourishing. From "needs improvement" teacher texts most days in the week—to almost never.

Sometimes the impact of embodied love is dramatic and immediate. Chris was in a group of men committed to the healing journey, in Jesus Christ. One evening, the brothers discussed how they received—or didn't receive—the love of God as a child. When it was his turn to share, Chris poured out his experience as a little boy, his struggle over the years as a man, husband, father—and what he still longed to understand about the Father's love . . . for him. While he was telling his story, another guy in the group named Dave stood up, crossed the room, and sat down next to Chris. Then Dave turned and pulled all 180 pounds of grown-man Chris onto his lap and held him, rocked him, stroked his brow, kissed him, and nurtured him . . . as if he was his infant son. While the eight other grown men in the room watched. Later, Dave said, "Hey bro, sorry if I was over the top," to which Chris responded, "You don't understand. I've been longing for someone to do that to me my entire life. *Today I felt the love of the Father like I've never felt it before.*"

Chris had heard the words "the Father loves you" many times, even from me in numerous sermons and Bible studies. But for the love of God to land more deeply in his spirit, words about God's love needed flesh. What I ache for each of you to understand is that this wasn't a unique, intended-to-be-rare body of Christ moment. Embodied love was ancient-church normal—bringing the healing power of the resurrected Christ to the sin and pain of our forefathers and mothers (Romans 12:3-21; 1 Peter 4:8-11). Today, many of us are locked down in wound and sin because, know it or not, we're starving for more than a sermon and a song—longing for a love we can see, feel, and touch that will infiltrate our spirit in a place mere words cannot reach—to heal us, transform us, and set us free.

And for those who are nervous about being hauled onto someone's lap, embodied love doesn't always need to be quite that intense! Often, *the healing love of Jesus is experienced through simple, focused presence.* Most of us are used to being overlooked, passed by—at work, home, church, in our circle of relationships—not valuable enough for someone else to focus on for an instant. We feel irrelevant. Unnecessary. Expendable. Love that heals the suffering of isolation is love that says, "I'm here. I'm with you. You matter."

This is how Jesus is with us. Fully present, his eyes gazing into ours. Listening carefully to every word we speak. Never bored. Never distracted. Tuned in because he loves us. And every second we spend together, we're less broken, more whole—because *when Jesus is simply present, his powerful love begins to heal.* In the same way, when we come together in our brokenness and sin, and are *simply present to one another with the love of Jesus,* hell trembles. Because, my brothers and sisters, we are the body of the resurrected King, the Lord Jesus Christ. We must never, ever forget.

A few years ago, I walked into Hope Community Church on a Sunday morning as a member of the congregation, having preached my last sermon a few months earlier. Carla was out of town, so I plopped down alone in one of the curved, century-old oak pews. Soon, David and his young family slipped in next to me. Our community rose together and began singing to the God we love, and in a few moments, I was suppressing sobs. At first, I wasn't sure what was happening—but then I knew. My final sermon at Hope was also my final sermon as lead pastor anywhere. Worshiping with my safe Hope family that morning released a vault of overwhelming emotion—a complex mixture of over three decades of joys and sorrows—that I thought I had already felt and released. As we sang, thousands of God's sons and daughters I had been honored to serve waltzed across the landscape of my spirit. When we finally sat down, I continued to weep, head in my hands. Slowly, my friend David slid over, put his arm around me, and gently drew my head to his shoulder. No words. David was simply present—holding me with the love of Jesus. And my grieving heart began to heal.

Now, the rest of the story. David was an extremely gifted young man and a serious believer who for years had been fighting a sexual addiction that drew him toward unsafe liaisons with men. Our church family knew about David's struggle—he and his wife had shared some of their story in our community of wounded healers because they desperately needed brothers and sisters to love and walk with them. David told me he woke up that particular Sunday morning incredibly tempted to act out—but instead he prayed, "Father, you know my heart longs for appropriate love and affection from good men, safe brothers in Christ. I'm not going out. I'm going to Hope. Would you meet my heart's need there?"

I hadn't been to Hope in weeks and never went without Carla. I was totally unaware of my struggle with ungrieved loss and unintentionally chose that particular pew to sit in that morning. David woke up to the shouts of his addiction and chose instead to trust and cry out for help. And then he bravely drew close to me, with no clue that my need for compassion would meet his need for a safe brother. But Jesus knew. He knew about all of it. He always knows—because we are his body. And part of his plan is to heal us . . . through us . . . all the way home.

"Many days alone along life's pathway" is death. But "we are the body of Christ" is life. Right now, in the name of Jesus, send your isolation—in all its forms—back to the hell it came from. Then, take off your mask, embrace your brothers and sisters, and walk together into the power and freedom of the abiding life.

Chapter 9

HEALING FROM SHAME

Looking unto Jesus, the author and finisher of our faith, who for the joy
that was set before Him endured the cross, despising the shame, and has
sat down at the right hand of the throne of God.

HEBREWS 12:2

[Shame] is the primary tool that evil leverages,
out of which emerges everything that we would call sin.
The healing of shame begins and ends in the experience of being known. . . .

DR. CURT THOMPSON

Spiritual transformation does not result from fixing our problems. It results
from turning to God in the midst of them and meeting God just as we are. . . .
Turning to God in our sin and shame is the heart of spiritual transformation.

DR. DAVID BENNER

Abiding in Jesus' love calls us to heal
from shame—through courageous
vulnerability met by the love of God.

"GIRLS, I'M AFRAID I HAVE SOME BAD NEWS," I whispered to Andrea, Leigh Anne, and Caroline, who met us at the back door on a warm June Saturday afternoon. I was heartsick. I was the lead pastor at a large suburban-like church on Detroit's east side, and Carla and I had just returned from a hastily called meeting with our elders. Andrea was graduating from high school that weekend, so her grandparents were parked in our living room. Needing privacy, I led us upstairs to Andrea's bedroom, where our small family gathered in an intimate

143

circle. I took a moment to breathe, "Please help me, Father," and then braved the dreaded words: "I just got fired."

Every molecule of oxygen was instantly sucked from the room. Andrea and Leigh Anne began to sob loudly in disbelief while Caroline, my eleven-year-old, stood frozen in place, silently weeping. I will never forget the pain. Soon, both Carla and I were crying, holding onto our girls and one another. Time stood still. My degrees, experience, and leadership skills couldn't prepare me for that moment, and I remember feeling clueless about what should come next. Then, I knew. We knelt around Andrea's bed, and amid our muffled sobs, I staggered through a desperate prayer: "Father, we're broken, confused, hurt, and afraid. We don't know what to do. But we love you, and we believe you love us and are with us. So, if you will show us the way, and give us courage, we promise to follow you. Through Jesus Christ, our Lord." Then, we slowly picked ourselves up, wiped our tears, and walked—together—down the stairs into the rest of our lives. That afternoon each of us began a long, difficult journey from brokenness to healing. For me, it would mean a return pilgrimage through the shadowy valley of shame.

Shame is the darkness that overwhelmed me eleven years earlier, when I almost ended my life on a Detroit expressway. Let me be clear—I'm not referring to a redemptive kind of shame sometimes mentioned in Scripture: a humbling, necessary sense that we're human, sinful, and in need of God. No, this is a devastating, exhausting, hopeless kind of shame—spawned by years of dysfunctional family and "just do it" Christianity—that told me I was less than human and unredeemable, and that no matter how hard I tried, I would never be enough. That Saturday in June, unhealthy shame roared back into my life.

The Scripture is clear—our enemy is not playing. He hates us and wants us dead. When Jesus said, "The thief comes only to steal and kill and destroy" (John 10:10, ESV), he meant it. John calls Satan "the accuser of our brothers and sisters . . . day and night" (Revelation 12:10, NLT). So, no matter how many victories we win in our battle with the powers of darkness—even over shame—Satan's mantra is always, "Wait till next time." He never sleeps, never stops stalking us—he hovers, patiently waiting for just one more opportunity to bring us to ruin.

Shame isn't a secondary concern—since the events of Genesis 3, it has been Satan's primary weapon against the sons and daughters of God. Literally everything we've discussed in previous chapters about abiding in the love of Jesus is dependent on us defeating shame.

The reason shame is so powerful? *Because it speaks to the core of our identity.* Shame is not only the sense that we're not enough—but that we're tragically different. Irreparably damaged. Unworthy of love. "When you experience shame," psychologist Sandra Wilson says, "it is as if you are standing alone on one side of a broken bridge while everyone else in the world stares at you from the other side."[1] And most importantly—shame is different from guilt, and the differences are eye-opening:

> > Guilt is about what I do—shame is about who I am.
> > Guilt tells me I made a mistake. Shame shouts that I *am* a mistake.
> > Guilt can be forgiven—shame orders me to cease to exist.[2]

Have you ever sinned and, overwhelmed by guilt, confessed your sin to God, trusting Scripture's promise that he always forgives (1 John 1:9)? Then, surprisingly, you still wanted to crawl in a hole, hide, disappear? My friend—that's shame. An action can be forgiven, but how can we be forgiven for *existing*?

Many of us have at least occasionally wrestled with that free-floating sense of *My whole life is one big screwup*, or *I will never get it right*, or *No one could love someone like me*—driven to hide behind performance, humor, anger, money, addiction, hypervigilance, violence, sadness, or even some warped version of Christianity. Shame makes us believe that if our real selves come out of hiding, we will be rejected. Shame shouts to our spirit, day and night, "No one loves you. You're alone. You have no hope. Be afraid. Hide. Cease to exist. Every day of your miserable life."

Make no mistake, shame isn't simply trying to slow us down or distract us. Shame wants our very selves to die. This is the bottom line, my brothers and sisters: *Shame is the satanic antithesis of God's love.* If the love of God heals, fills, and frees us to partner with the resurrected Jesus in his battle for humanity—shame assaults, cripples, and enslaves us, causing us to be both personally miserable and Kingdom ineffective. Psychiatrist Curt Thompson's words are paradigm altering:

> [Shame] is used . . . to dismantle us as individuals and communities, and destroy all of God's creation.
>
> [Shame] is *the primary tool that evil leverages*, out of which emerges everything that we would call sin.[3]

In other words, we don't sin in a vacuum, or just because we're born with what theologians call a "sin nature." We choose sin under the influence of a deadly, spiritual toxin called shame. God loves us and created us to respond most naturally to his love (John 14:23), and while we can foolishly choose to disobey despite his love—his love never, ever gives us reason to disobey. Only shame beckons us toward the darkness. In forty years of multigenerational, multicultural ministry, I've seen it all—addiction, broken marriages, racial hatred, misogyny, sexual wound, violence, anxiety, insecurity, arrogance, deep sadness, religious rigidity, and every kind of relational wound and abuse imaginable—and I'm convinced that every ounce of this sin and pain can be traced, in some way, back to shame.

This means that whenever you hear a shaming voice in your spirit—*You're worthless* or *I'm just about done with you* or *Will you ever get your act together?*—you can be sure it isn't the voice of God but of Satan masquerading as God. Dear brother or sister, you may be overwhelmed by a torturous, deafening choir of shaming voices even now. Please know—your heavenly Father loves you too much to ever speak to you like that. Even when the Father deals with us sternly, speaking words of discipline—which sometimes he must— it's impossible to miss his love. A few weeks before I was fired, I remember contemplating the church's success during my tenure and arrogantly saying to myself, *They can't fire me; I built this place.* I'm embarrassed that at the time, I couldn't see my own hubris and was oblivious to how far, in that area of my spirit, I had drifted from the heart of Jesus. In any case, months later, God's voice gently but clearly whispered, "I need to tell you something, son. I heard your words that day, and I saw your pride. It was then that I decided to allow you to be deeply wounded . . . because I love you." Stern, difficult words. But words of love, not shame, that called me to deeper obedience as a man, husband, and father.

Our first and most important battleground against shame? Childhood. Shame is transmitted primarily through *shame-based family systems*. If our child hearts receive the parental love we're created for, we flourish—and begin to be drawn to an even Greater Love that will fill us "with all the fullness of God" (Ephesians 3:19, NRSV). But if the love we desperately need is absent, love's opposite—shame—*immediately occupies love's place in our spirit.* Even as infants, something inside us begins to shrivel and die. In fact, neurobiologists tell us that a baby can feel the impact of love—or unlove—as early as the third trimester in the womb.[4] If parents struggle to know the love of God, all they have left to give is shame, in its various deadly forms. We cannot give away what we haven't received. Psychologist Robert Karen says it plainly: "[Shame] is frequently instilled at a delicate age, as the result of the internalization of a contemptuous voice, usually parental."[5]

Performance-based parenting, lack of affection, emotional distance—all can download shame into our children. But most often, children absorb shame's "contemptuous voice" from our own unhealed shame embedded in the way we discipline. One Sunday when the girls were little, I preached a sermon on shame and asked Andrea and Leigh Anne to role-play with me. In the first service, I played the loud, finger-pointing, angry, shaming dad, and Andrea was stellar as the victimized daughter. It was great fun, our community loved it—and the spiritual point was driven home. The second service was a different story. About five minutes into our role-play, as I stood tall over five-year-old Leigh Anne, glaring angrily, raising my voice in dismissive shame . . . my precious little girl looked up at me, eyes brimming with tears, and said, "Daddy, I don't want to do this anymore." I immediately dropped to my knees, took her in my arms, and choking back repentant sobs whispered, "It's okay, baby. I'm so sorry. We're done." Our Sunday-morning "drama" had become, in Leigh Anne's mind, a reenactment, triggering memories of my real-life, shame-based parenting.

Thankfully, because of the healing work of Jesus Christ in my life, my girls received not only shame but a great deal of the Father's love over the course of their childhood. On Father's Day three years ago, my grown-up Caroline wrote, "When I think of you, Dad, I think of love. You've taught me so much over the years . . . but what stands out most to me is how you've been a consistent and pure example of love—loving oneself, loving others, and receiving the love of Jesus." When I first read her words, I thought, *Sweetie, thanks, but you must be mistaken. Don't you remember when you were three and I shamed you over the spilled juice box? Or when you were ten and I wouldn't let you get off the couch until you prayed out loud in our family prayer time? Or when you were sixteen and I shouted you down at the kitchen table for being so stubborn? Because that's what I remember.* It's the nature of shame to focus on failure as proof that "I'm a loser." But once more, Peter's words ring powerfully true: "Love will cover a multitude of sins" (1 Peter 4:8). As I continued to battle my own shame through the love of Christ, his redeeming love began to slowly transform my parenting and even heal past shame damage in Caroline—so that what she remembers most today is how much I loved her.

So, if you're a parent, be encouraged. If the love of Jesus Christ can do this in me—one of the most shame-based dads I've ever met—he can do this in and through you. Your parenting journey isn't about perfection but gut-level honesty about where you are with shame right now. No matter where you find yourself, you can respond to the Father's voice as he says, "Son, daughter—you don't need to live this way anymore. I love you. Let me begin to heal you and set you free."

Nevertheless, if a child's life is permeated by shame—and maybe this was *your* reality when *you* were a child—*the impact is devastating.* So many of us carry unhealed childhood shame—from family, society, even the church. When the girls were small, we would often pile into the La-Z-Boy and watch *Mr. Rogers' Neighborhood* together. Remember the lyrics to his famous song? "It's you I like, / It's not the things you wear, / It's not the way you do your hair / But it's you I like . . . / The way down deep inside you / Not the things that hide you . . . / But it's you I like / Every part of you."[6] One afternoon, as I listened with all three girls curled up on my lap, a few small tears journeyed down my face. "Look, Daddy's crying. Why are you crying, Daddy?" Leigh Anne asked, touching my tears as if to verify their reality.

"I'm not sure, sweetheart," I replied. And at the time, I didn't have a clue why this slender, soft-spoken man and his goofy little song would move me so deeply. But today I know. The little boy inside my strong, ex-footballer, weight lifter, grown-man body had been so wounded by shame and was still trying to heal—and longed for someone to say those words to him. I wanted someone, anyone— maybe especially God—to tell me not only that they loved me but that they liked me. The real me, warts and all. Truth be told, isn't that what we all want?

I'm sure you have your own story of shame declaring "you'll never be enough"—whether because of gender, race, sexuality, your spiritual journey, the way you look, or where you live. Satan uses all available criteria to make us feel anything but the life-giving love of God. No wonder so many of us muddle along, day after day, locked down in varying degrees of shame. Some might counter, "At least I'm functional." Fair enough. But know this, dear friend—Jesus Christ didn't endure the Cross so we could be functional. Jesus died to "set us free" (Galatians 5:1, ESV).

What would it be like for you to take a courageous step toward freedom right now, getting honest about your past—and contemplating signs of residual shame lurking in your spirit today? Here's a list of some of shame's markers. Each comes not from a textbook but from my own journey of battling shame. Which of these reflect an area where shame has wounded—and locked down—your spirit?

> *Wrestling with identity—or self-hatred.* We struggle to know and accept who God has created us, uniquely, to be. Some of us even secretly battle self-hatred. Serious followers of Jesus can hate themselves. I know . . . because I did.

> *Tormented by voices from childhood.* How can we hear the Father's voice, "You are my beloved son, my beloved daughter, in whom I am well-pleased"—when the voices from our past never stop shouting their shame?

> *Constantly looking for approval.* Everyone needs encouragement—but shame addicts us to outside affirmation because we're not sure how to receive God's reassuring words of love deep in our hearts.

> *Critical of others.* Our internal critic relentlessly spouts false beliefs to our hearts—*I'm damaged goods. If I'm my true self, people will not want to be my friend. I don't fit with anyone, anywhere*—criticism we, in turn, give away to others.

> *Arrogance.* Sometimes those who brag, boast, and even bully others do so unconsciously to hide the deep shame they feel but aren't sure how to handle.

> *Difficulty in relationships.* Often this is because we unconsciously put pressure on a spouse, child, or friend to fill the emptiness inside—which only the love of God is designed to fill.

> *Never at peace—constantly driven.* Staying busy keeps the shaming voices at bay. We're scared to slow down because if we do, we'll be forced to deal with our pain.

> *Struggling with addiction.* Not just alcohol, drugs, or sex but anything, including work, money, success, recreation,

relationships—even spirituality—that takes over our life in a futile attempt to put salve on hearts broken by shame.

> *Disappointment in our relationship with God.* Shame causes us to doubt God's love and believe he looks at us with constant disapproval. Why would we want to spend time with him if we're convinced we will never, ever measure up?

Each of these markers reflects struggle with ourselves, with others, or with God (Matthew 22:34-40). In other words: *Shame destroys relationships.* When we live in shame, we can't love God or receive his love—or love and receive love from others—because we're overwhelmed by unworthiness. Where shame rules, we can't love our brothers and sisters in Christ, let alone our enemies. Because we refuse to love one another, our broken world also bleeds out with division—racial hatred and violence, rampant abortion, war, broken family systems, and more. The world doesn't come to Jesus Christ not because we haven't found the right evangelism strategy but because shame has siphoned Christ's love from our hearts. Shame stops the Kingdom of God in its tracks. And it must be defeated.

Can we win this battle with shame? Without question! But before I tell you *how,* it's crucial that I tell you *why.* We have power over shame because Jesus not only battled and overcame shame his entire life but decisively defeated shame at the Cross.

Remember, Jesus was fully human, "made in every respect like us, his brothers and sisters" (Hebrews 2:17, NLT). But sometimes we forget that "sameness" includes battling shame. Satan's first recorded words to Jesus are the repeated, shaming taunt, "*If* You are the Son of God" (Matthew 4:1-11). The religious leaders publicly allude to the possibility of Jesus' culturally shameful illegitimate birth—"*We're* not bastards"

(John 8:39-41, MSG, emphasis added)—a rumor that followed him everywhere. Jesus' friends were those whom polite, religious society looked down on with shame—tax collectors, prostitutes, and the marginalized, diseased, and broken (Luke 5:30; 15:2). Jesus himself was labeled a shameful partier, a drunk (Luke 7:34). Isaiah prophesies first-century Israel's response to such an unremarkable, dismissable man:

> There was nothing beautiful or majestic about his appearance,
>   nothing to attract us to him.
> He was despised and rejected—
>   a man of sorrows, acquainted with deepest grief.
> We turned our backs on him and looked the other way.
>   He was despised, and we did not care.
>
> ISAIAH 53:2-3, NLT

And then Jesus faced the shame of the cross. Early in Israel's history, Moses declared, "Cursed is everyone who is hung on a tree" (Galatians 3:13, NLT; see also Deuteronomy 21:23). For the Romans as well, the cross wasn't just an instrument of pain but of shame. Only the vilest criminals—the lowest of the low—went to the cross. The condemned were stripped before being spiked to their personal tree of death, then crucified near trafficked areas where they could be seen and mocked—as Jesus was—by religious leaders and regular folk. Even those crucified next to him took their turn (Matthew 27:39-44). In other words, the Son of God courageously embraced his death naked, in shame, for you and for me (John 19:2-3).

As Jesus faced the cross, hell's shame bellowed one last time, "Turn back!" But Jesus shouted "Never!" and because of love, pressed on to his death for you, for me, for the world. The author of Hebrews says it like this:

Jesus, the founder and perfecter of our faith, who for the
joy that was set before him endured the cross, *despising the
shame*, and is seated at the right hand of the throne of God.

HEBREWS 12:2, ESV, EMPHASIS ADDED

When Jesus breathed his last, the death-dealing shame that had
plagued God's sons and daughters since Adam and Eve was defeated.
Forever. *When Jesus calls us to abide in his love, he's calling us to walk in
the same power that crushed shame at the Cross.* The only power shame
has in our lives today is the power we give it.

As I walk in Jesus' love and pour out my shame . . . he doesn't
just hear me, he feels with me (Hebrews 4:15). When I experience
rejection, he whispers, "I know. You're not alone." When I feel deeply
inadequate, he pulls me close, saying, "I've been there, son. Let me
take some of that burden and give you the security of my love in
exchange." What if this experienced solidarity with the Son of God is
intended to be a part of the arsenal we bring to the fight when Satan
begins to bombard us with shame? What if Jesus' words, "My peace
I give to you. . . . Let not your heart be troubled, neither let it be
afraid" (John 14:27), applied even to our battle with shame? What if
we learned to say to hell's accusing voice, "Jesus the resurrected Christ
has already endured the earthly onslaught of your shame and won,
and *he now stands with me—and his love covers me.* Go back to hell
where you came from—and take your shame with you."

The powerful love and work of Jesus is why we can defeat shame—
and that brings us back full circle, to the question of how . . . and
to my story. On the day I got fired, and for the next few long, difficult years, my battle wasn't with mistakes I made in ministry—those
could be repented and forgiven. I wrestled with the overwhelming
feeling that what was being rejected was *me*. That I was unloved

because I had failed to perform. That after years of ministry success, the curtain had been pulled back, and I was exposed as a sham. The crippling narrative of shame.

The worst part of the nightmare? Seeing the hurt in my girls. I was their hero. Shame shouted, *You failed them. They'll never look at you the same way again.* They faced rumors at school about what their dad had done to get fired—all untrue. The firing revolved around pushback from leadership against my passion to see racial justice realized in our church. But still, more shame. I struggled to show my face in public because I couldn't deal with the stares. I wanted to leave ministry forever—not only because I no longer trusted Christians but because I felt tarnished, tainted, unfit. One night I woke up sobbing, "Carla, I know I made mistakes, but please tell me I'm not a bad man. Please tell me God still loves me." All she could do was hold me.

Then one day the doorbell rang—and there stood Bill, one of my dearest friends. I was dumbfounded because Bill was from Dallas, had a family, was the pastor of an active church—and he hadn't told me he was coming! "What are you doing here, bro?" I asked.

Bill compassionately replied, "I love you, Kev. I wasn't going to let you go through this alone." I don't remember how long Bill stayed—but he went with me to a post-firing elder meeting, advocating for me when I was too full of shame to advocate for myself. Then, early one morning, Bill came downstairs and held me while I wept out more shame—like Carla had days before. No words. Just the embrace of brotherly love, which not only secured me in the moment but also brought healing from Jesus Christ that enabled me to take one more step toward wholeness. In fact, without the timely love of Jesus in and through my brother Bill—and Ed, Carlton, Lawrence, Ron, and many, many others—I would still be locked down in shame's darkness, a dead man walking.

Here's what I need you to hear: When it comes to shame, the same is true for you. Your shame cannot be privately wished away. It needs healing. *Vulnerability met by the powerful, embodied love of Jesus Christ heals us and sets us free*[7]—even from hell's most devastating weapon. Of course, this vulnerability is crucial in our personal relationship with Jesus. We heal as we get honest with him about our shame and learn to hear his words of love in reply. But we need the love of our brothers and sisters in Christ, as well—and they can't embrace us with his healing love unless we're willing to risk revealing the shame we've been hiding. Think about it—if you tell me you love me, but I haven't let you see the real me, I know you're loving a caricature. For Christ's love in you to heal me, I need to know you're loving who I really am. I must let you see me.

But getting honest about shame is even more difficult than getting honest about garden-variety sin and woundedness. So, when I'm teaching about shame's healing in a retreat setting, I use an exercise to help folks have courage to take a step toward vulnerability. Everyone receives a blank cardboard mask—and then they're asked to write on the front of their mask what they want everyone to believe about them—and on the back of their mask, to note what they hide about themselves, what they don't want anyone to know or see. Then, I lead the way by sharing my own mask. On the front, "I want you to believe that . . ."

> I have it all together.
> I'm tireless.
> I'm fully healed from childhood wounds.
> I never doubt God or myself.
> My anger issues are completely in the past.

> > I trust God completely with my kids and grandkids.
> > I'm a great pray-er—and understand the whole Bible.
> > Fights with Carla are rare—and always end with Communion and the Lord's Prayer.

But then, on the back . . .

> > I miss my girls terribly and shed tears over them . . . a lot.
> > I fear losing one of them—and am afraid my faith wouldn't survive.
> > I have big problems with God over why he doesn't heal more people physically.
> > Sometimes the pain around me and in the world is so intense, I doubt God's existence for a second.
> > I often doubt my effectiveness in ministry.
> > I'm exhausted after almost forty years as a pastor—sometimes I think I missed my calling and should have been a police officer.
> > I think I swear too much.
> > If I let myself, I think I could abuse alcohol—I don't, but I think I could.

I usually feel spiritually and emotionally naked after disclosing my shame—and a little afraid, because I know how judgmental and dismissive some of us can be. But I also know appropriate disclosure with close brothers and sisters in Christ is the only pathway to healing and freedom. I'll never forget watching three hundred men at an Arizona retreat a few years back, in small clusters, sharing the back of their "masks" with their brothers—decades of woundedness, sin, and shame hidden because of fear of rejection. Such a sacred moment—strong sons of God pouring out their truth, compassionately listening to one another, and then sobbing tears of relief, acceptance, and joy in one another's arms. I watched the healing love of Jesus Christ crush shame as heaven's freedom overpowered hell's bondage—on the spot.

Of course, a healing moment begins a healing journey, because long-term release from deeply entrenched shame takes time. But, if we stay the course, Jesus' love slowly silences shame's lies until one day our hearts finally, miraculously begin to believe, *God really loves me!*

That's my friend Ethan's story. Raised in an extremely conservative Christian home, Ethan was loved but also felt overwhelmed by fear . . . and shame. He was obsessively warned against every possible behavioral pitfall in a young man's life. Beware the JCPenney catalog because the women's section might cause lust. Premarital sex guarantees both a life and marriage disappointing to God—and probable ruin. One sip of alcohol and you'll become an alcoholic. Bowling or the movies could entice you to "love the world." The result? Underneath his smiling, gifted, smooth persona lived a hypervigilant, emotionally shutdown, performance-based young man, living on the edge of despair.

"For a long time," Ethan told me, "I didn't really get how messed up all of this was. In high school, my iron-fisted resolve was to live righteously in every area of my life until finally, exhausted, I broke down physically and emotionally. I got so sick I even had to drop out of sports—and one day I found myself in a cornfield on our farm, on my hands and knees, weeping, pounding my fist in the mud, wanting to die."

When Ethan got to college, he upped his performance game—"I was obsessed with meeting the standard I thought Christ set"—and also slipped into pornography "to numb the pain of having to grip my relationship with God so tightly." Eventually he met a girl, fell in love, and married—but his wife's sexually broken past triggered childhood lies. He said, "I was deeply ashamed I couldn't forgive her—but also haunted by the false belief that my chance for the happiness God promises 'the truly righteous' was gone forever. I couldn't love Emily, I hated myself, and I knew nothing about loving God. I was suicidal for months—and the breaking point came the night Emily found me in the living room, with a shotgun, ready to end everything."

Emily called that evening—not just because I was Ethan's pastor, but because she knew we'd been walking together in a group with ten other guys where Ethan had vulnerably wept, raged, cussed, despaired, questioned, studied, and prayed with us for months. I dialed Ethan's cell—"I love you, son, but you need to get help right now, or some of the brothers and I are on our way to take you to the hospital." That night, the truth about Jesus' love finally began to break through. "I started seeing a doctor and a therapist," Ethan told me, "but it was Emily's consistent love and acceptance, along with the love of the men who walked with me all those months—that finally helped me emerge from my dark night. Today I finally get it—Jesus doesn't give a rip about my performance. But he longs for me to know how much he loves me. For the first time ever, I have some peace and joy—and I'm learning to love and serve others not out of obligation but because I'm loved."

Ethan was one of the most shame-saturated young men I had ever met. Today, he is beginning to experience the freedom of the abiding life. But his healing has taken—and continues to take—time. So has mine. So will yours. Our enemy will even shame us about our slow progress healing from shame! But don't be discouraged. Remember, you are a son, a daughter of the living God. You walk in the powerful love of the resurrected Jesus. You are a warrior for his Kingdom—a wounded healer taking his healing love into the broken world around you. Stay on the healing path. Jesus is with you. He loves you with all of his heart—and because his love covers you and empowers you, shame cannot win. "My peace I give to you. . . . Let not your heart be troubled," Jesus said. You are slowly being made whole. You, too, are starting to experience the freedom of the abiding life.

Chapter 10

SHARING OUR GREAT LOVE
WITH A BROKEN WORLD

Be imitators of God as dear children. And walk in love,
as Christ also has loved us and given Himself for us.

EPHESIANS 5:1-2

Jesus, at his ascension, was given by the creator God an empire built on
love. As we ourselves open our lives to the warmth of that love, we begin
to lose our fear . . . we begin to become people through whom the power of
that love can flow out into the world around that so badly needs it.

N. T. WRIGHT

Execute judgment and righteousness, and deliver the plundered out of
the hand of the oppressor. Do no wrong and do no violence to the stranger,
the fatherless, or the widow.

JEREMIAH 22:3

[We need] leaders not in love with money, but in love with justice; leaders
not in love with publicity, but in love with humanity.

MARTIN LUTHER KING, JR.

Abiding in Jesus' love calls us to a sacrificial
lifestyle of radical love that compels the world
to come home to him.

SEVERAL MONTHS AGO, I arrived early at the Detroit airport and
decided to have dinner before my flight. My server was efficient and
polite but distant—and I began to tune in to what I sensed was a

sadness she carried as she moved from table to table. I felt overwhelming empathy for this daughter of God; there was no way I was going to head for my gate until I risked asking about her real life. Twenty minutes later, I called for the check, left a tip, and made my way to the front entrance, where I asked the host if he could find my waitress so I could speak with her. When she arrived, I said, "Miss, thank you so much for serving me—you were great! Would you allow me to share one thought with you before I catch my plane?" She nodded yes, so I continued, "I felt a deep sadness in you this evening. I have no idea what's going on in your life, but I believe in a God who loves us so much—who loves *you* so much—and I think he wants you to know he sees you, he knows all about what is burdening you, he cares deeply, and he is with you. You are not alone."

I slipped her an extra twenty and whispered, "God bless you." And then, in a flash, she began to sob. Her hands flew to her face, and she sprinted out the entrance and around the corner toward the airport ladies' room. The restaurant host shot me a *What just happened?* look. But I'm fairly certain I know what happened. Just beneath the surface of this precious daughter of God's everyday life, she lived in significant pain—convinced no one saw, no one knew, no one cared. Then she discovered—*God sees her*. And *the profound, comforting truth that she wasn't invisible, unloved, or alone* bypassed her defenses and touched her in deeply wounded places in her spirit. I have no clue about this young woman's faith journey before that moment, and I deeply regret that I couldn't wait for her return due to my soon-departing flight. But I promise you this—on an otherwise unremarkable evening in a crowded airport restaurant, the Father's love and compassion embraced his daughter—and began to draw her home.

It's called . . . evangelism.

You might say, "Wait. You didn't tell her about Jesus, his death and resurrection, forgiveness of sin, or eternity. You spent zero time convincing her that her previous belief system was false. And you didn't lead her in a sinner's prayer, or hear her public confession of faith. What kind of evangelism is that?" Fair question. But what if much of what we have believed about evangelism is at best misguided and at worst, flat-out wrong—hindering, not helping our broken world come to Jesus?

I believe in Jesus Christ, his death, resurrection, forgiveness of sin, and eternal life. I affirm the ancient creeds of Christ's church—and believe more than ever that everyone on the planet needs to know Jesus; that no one experiences real life outside of him; and that all sin, pain, and death in the world longs to be forgiven and healed through his love and grace. I'm passionate about the church of Jesus Christ sharing him with everyone, everywhere. *If*, that is, we're sharing the real Jesus and *if* the way we're proclaiming him represents him well.

The word *evangelism* simply means "to proclaim good news."[1] In fact, our word *gospel* comes from the Anglo-Saxon word "gods-pel"—which means "good story" or "good news."[2] In the first century, "good news" was often associated with a new ruler whose reign promised peace and prosperity to all who pledged their allegiance. An inscription found in Turkey dated to 9 BC refers to the birthday of Caesar Augustus (the emperor of the Roman Empire when Jesus was born) as "for the whole world the beginning of the good news."[3] So when Mark titles his biography "This is the Good News about Jesus the Messiah, the Son of God" (Mark 1:1, NLT), he was boldly proclaiming to the ancient world, "there's a new sheriff in town," inviting everyone to compare the emperor's good news with the good news of Jesus of Nazareth. But what we sometimes forget is that Mark's "good news" about Jesus . . . *is Jesus*.

Of course, Jesus' good news involves certain crucial historical and theological details about his life and teaching—especially his death and resurrection—that define him and his mission. Otherwise, we're inviting people to believe in a Jesus who is nothing more than a bundle of nice, religious ideas—no different from any other prophet in history and truly "good news" to no one. But what matters more than anything else is that Jesus *himself* is the answer to humanity's presenting issue: the sin that rewards us with horrifying pain and death and that separates us from God and true life. We desperately long for a deliverer to do for us what we cannot do for ourselves— break down the sin barrier and bring us home. To this longing, Jesus offers . . . himself. "He who believes *in Me* has everlasting life," Jesus announces to his spiritually hungry audience in Galilee (John 6:47, emphasis added). Just before he left the planet, he reminded his disciples, "You shall be witnesses *to Me* in Jerusalem, and in all Judea and Samaria, and to the end of the earth" (Acts 1:8, emphasis added). Paul's words to the ancient church of Colossae leave no room for doubt: "We preach *Christ*, warning people not to add to the Message" (Colossians 1:26-29, MSG).

This means, first of all, that Jesus' "good news" is not Christianity. Not fourth-century Christianity or Reformation Christianity or Orthodox, Baptist, Methodist, Pentecostal, or Roman Catholic Christianity. I deeply appreciate elements of each of these historical traditions. They work hard to represent Jesus well. But when I share the good news of Jesus with a follower of Islam, a Buddhist, or an atheist, I'm not trying to convince them of an alternative "ism." Yes, Peter calls us to "be ready to give a defense . . . for the hope that is in [us]" (1 Peter 3:15)—but our "hope" isn't Christianity. It's Jesus Christ. If my Jewish or Hindu friend wants to talk about the differences between our beliefs, I will oblige, but only so that somehow, he or she can see Jesus. In fact, when someone asks me about my faith, I never call myself a Christian. Instead I almost always reply, "I follow Jesus of Nazareth—and I love him."

The young woman in the airport restaurant wasn't looking for institutional religion. She wasn't looking for Christianity. But the moment her broken heart heard and felt the "good news" that God was personal, that he cared about her and her pain, she was drawn to him. If I only have a few moments with someone who doesn't know Jesus, that's the good news I'm going to tell them, every single time. Every moment spent compassionately communicating the good news of Jesus Christ and his love—verbally or nonverbally—to someone who doesn't know him is evangelism. Madeleine L'Engle says it beautifully,

> We draw people to Christ not by loudly discrediting what
> they believe, by telling them how wrong they are and how
> right we are, but by showing them a light that is so lovely
> that they want with all their hearts to know the source of it.[4]

Why is it, then, that we're so addicted to the "content" of the good news? For one, because the enemy has deceived us into believing that Jesus Christ can be captured—and most effectively shared—in some precise, correct theological statement about him and his life. The Apostle's Creed brilliantly articulates the person and work of Jesus, but there's a reason we don't regularly hand out copies to lead others to him. The power of Jesus' good news isn't in theologically accurate descriptions of him but in *him*—and especially the way he communicates *himself* through his intimate love relationship with each of us. When Jesus sent Peter out into the world to share the good news, he didn't ask him if he had learned his lesson after denying him or if

Peter now had a better theological understanding of who Jesus really was. Instead he simply asked, "Do you love me?" (John 21:15-17).

A few years back, in preparation for a talk on parenting, Carla and I e-mailed each of our grown daughters the question, "What stands out about the way we raised you that helped you believe in Jesus' love for you and eventually to put your faith in him?" The list was encouragingly long—"daddy-daughter dances, letting us climb in bed with you during a thunderstorm, seeing you fight through things in your marriage, allowing us to be ourselves, knowing you were always available"—and more. But at the end of her list, my middle daughter Leigh Anne said, "Mom and Dad, more than anything else, today I follow Jesus and know that he loves me because when we were kids, *you both showed me that you knew Jesus really loved you.*"

Listen, I bought my girls their first Bibles, took them to youth group, prayed with them every night, and had theological discussions with each of them about everything from the creation of the universe to Jesus coming back from the dead to "Hey Dad, how do we know what we believe is right?" All of it helped them find their way. But don't miss this: Leigh Anne eventually believed in Jesus and his love for her because she saw Jesus and his love even in our very imperfect lives. The power of the good news of Jesus Christ in the abiding life.

What then moves us to share Jesus in the first place is not guilt or shame but rather our love relationship with Jesus. In the freedom of loving him, we can release the false guilt of "not knowing enough," the fear of not having "the right answers," and especially the need to convince anyone of anything. His love creates a love and compassion for others and a passion to share him that cannot be stopped.

There's nothing intrinsically evil about scheduling a time to share the good news. Many campus ministries organize spring-break trips with a goal of hitting the beach and speaking truth about Jesus to as many people as possible. And because the good news is powerful in any form it's presented, some will believe. But this way of sharing Jesus reminds me more of trained cold-call salesmen and women going door to door, looking for buyers. At best, it feels unnatural and more confrontational than relational—and makes it more difficult to communicate the love we may genuinely feel.

Jesus' "heart broke" over the crowd gathered on a Galilean hillside because they were "like sheep with no shepherd" (Mark 6:32-34, MSG). He wept over Jerusalem because his brothers and sisters were drowning in their sin and pain (Luke 19:41). This I know—*when our hearts break for those who don't yet believe, shame-based, structured evangelism becomes obsolete*. Sales personnel eventually get tired and quit. Jesus' love moves his followers—a Kingdom army of lovers—to really see . . . and to share his good news with anyone, anywhere, anytime. All the way home.

The truth is, if we share Jesus Christ for any other reason than because we're moved by love for him *and* for the person with whom we're sharing, they will sense it and often will reject him because they feel like a recruit, a statistic, a "mark." A few years ago, I became friends with a Muslim sister, and for a time, we met regularly over coffee, discussing everything from family to the state of world affairs to religion. I'm ashamed to say that slowly, insidiously, I began to see my friend as someone to convert. Instead of allowing Jesus' love in me to produce a deep, long-term love for her—*whether she ever believed in Jesus as Messiah or not*—I began to get impatient, a sure sign of fading love (1 Corinthians 13:4, NLT). One day, as we were talking, I thought I saw an opening and tried to gently move her toward Jesus. My friend sensed I was trying to "save" her, and she was angry . . . but most of all, she was hurt. "Kevin," she interrupted, "I know what you're doing. I hope this isn't the reason why you've been meeting with me. I'm not going to become a Christian, so you need to stop." I had neither said nor done anything obvious—but my friend discerned an agenda other than love. After that day, we drifted apart and never spoke again. It broke my heart.

Abiding, making our home in God's love, is the unstoppable catalyst for sharing Jesus authentically and without agenda. But many of us still wonder, *Exactly what does someone need to know about Jesus in order to believe in him?* It's a difficult question to answer. How many details about my life—who I am and what I have done—would be necessary to communicate the essence of me? The same dilemma occurs when we share the person of Jesus.

My four-year-old Andrea was in the car with me when I dropped off a church leader at his home and said, "Take care, my brother." She immediately chimed in, "Daddy, he isn't your brother!" and I explained that we were special brothers because we both believed in Jesus. Without hesitation, her tender heart responded, "I believe in Jesus, Daddy!" I was overwhelmed with joy—but of course, wanted to make sure she wasn't simply saying what she thought her daddy wanted to hear. After a few questions, I was convinced that my little girl at some point before that moment, had quietly, without fanfare or formality, genuinely believed in Jesus. Her confession of faith was one of the greatest moments of my life.

But here's the deal: When Andrea believed, she didn't understand the Trinity, that Jesus was God in the flesh, what original sin was, or what the Cross meant. She wasn't even trying to figure out how to go to heaven! Andrea knew Jesus was good and kind and that he loved her—and somehow figured out she didn't just want him but needed him in her four-year-old life. Then, one day, my Andrea—*out of the need she felt*—*believed in the Jesus she understood.* Can you imagine Jesus saying, "Oh, sweetie, you can't believe in me quite yet—there's so much more you need to know about me before you can enter my Kingdom"? In fact, Jesus said quite the opposite. One day, with a little girl like Andrea in his arms, he pointedly remarked to his disciples, "Unless you accept God's kingdom in the simplicity of a child, you'll never get in" (Mark 10:13-16, MSG).

Ultimately, the gospel that *is Jesus* is the story of God loving us so much that he entered history *in Jesus* to deliver us from sin and death. Paul's words take my breath away: "He has rescued us from the kingdom of darkness and transferred us into the Kingdom of his dear Son, who purchased our freedom and forgave our sins" (Colossians 1:13-14, NLT). So, yes, the virgin birth, his miracles, the Cross, and the empty tomb and more are a part of the story that *is Jesus*. Nevertheless, our faith in everything Jesus did in his earthly ministry isn't what saves us. *Faith in Jesus saves us!* At the precise moment of believing, we may know a great deal about Jesus' person and work—or, like Andrea, we may know nothing more than that we need him. This, my friends, is the delicious, powerful, life-giving freedom of the good news: "For this is how God loved the world: He gave his one and only Son, so that everyone *who believes in him* will not perish but have eternal life" (John 3:16, NLT, emphasis added).

There's so much more we could say because there are so many areas of Jesus' gospel that, over the years, have been infected with a satanic virus—so many places where our enemy wants us to believe faith in Jesus isn't sufficient. Doubts about the quality or quantity of our faith—from hell. Our need to control when, how, or even if someone believes—from hell. Subtle additions to simple faith in Jesus—from hell. Connecting assurance of our faith to good works—from hell. On our worst days, when good works are nowhere to be found and we need assurance the most—our security can't be about who we are and what we have done but who he is and what he has done for us.

Even something as seemingly harmless as "asking someone to pray to receive Jesus" can be a tool of the enemy. Which prayer? What words? How do I know if I prayed correctly? All used by hell to draw attention away from Jesus' simple, freeing promise—"The one who believes in me . . . will live" (John 11:25-26, MSG). Most nonbelievers believe Jesus' good news isn't good news at all—simply an invitation to embrace a moral code they know they cannot keep and not that different from every other religion in the world. When we shout with our words and lives—"Jesus loves you and offers you eternal life . . . freely"—many broken sons and daughters will come home.

There is yet one more core component of New Testament evangelism, one we only sometimes dabble in and don't usually talk about. In fact, we often ignore it because it's simply . . . too hard. But it's directly from Jesus. He said to his disciples, his last night on the planet, "Love each other. Just as I have loved you . . . Your love for one another will *prove to the world that you are my disciples.*" A few hours later, he asked the Father, "I am praying . . . for all who will ever believe in me . . . that they will all be one, just as you and I are one . . . *so that the world will believe you sent me*" (John 13:34-35; 17:20-21, NLT, emphasis added).

While we focus on individuals trickling into God's Kingdom, Jesus has his eyes on the whole world, envisioning a living image of himself shining into the darkness, everywhere at once. This living image is his community of followers, the church, bound together across every line of division because of his love. Most astounding, Jesus promises if we love one another like this, the world will have unmistakable proof that he is *the One* sent by God to deliver us all.

And yet, today, Christianity is divided into over forty thousand different denominations, groups, and organizations, split over theology, race, ethnicity, class, politics, culture, and worship style.[5] Multicultural churches are sadly considered by many a special, optional kind of church for those who feel led—instead of just church, the way Jesus prayed it would be.

But how else do we interpret Paul's words about the church "where there is neither Greek nor Jew, circumcised nor uncircumcised, barbarian, Scythian, slave nor free, but Christ is all and in all" (Colossians 3:10-11). Does that sound optional to you? No! The church is meant to be a new kind of community where we "die to old identities and . . . come alive . . . to the new one, the solidarity of the Messiah."[6]

For those of us who believe the good news of Jesus is simply about how to get to heaven, Jesus' and Paul's words might not make much sense. But remember, since Adam and Eve, sin has not only separated us from God but from one another. And because God is so intensely relational, and we're created in his image, the most severe wounds we experience are relational. We bleed out every day over damaged relationships with spouses, children, parents, close friends—and even the neighbor next door. Since the beginning of time, we have desperately longed for healing.

So, when God's Deliverer, Jesus, came to earth to set things right, he not only bridged the gap between us and God but also broke down all hostility between us and our estranged human siblings. Paul says, "Christ brought us together through his death on the cross" (Ephesians 2:16-18, MSG). Enduring unspeakable hostility, Jesus himself literally became "our peace" (Ephesians 2:14, NRSV), rescuing us from the prison of devasting relational conflict and division.

Here's what we must not miss: Jesus envisioned his church displaying this longed-for relational healing to the world, a healing found *nowhere else in culture or history*, knowing the world would take notice. Imagine someone observing, "Wait, war is rampant, racial hatred is everywhere, I can't get my son to talk to me, my ex-husband hates me, and I just parted ways with my best friend—but your church has black folks, white folks, Latinos, and Asians, poor and rich, city and suburb, Republicans and Democrats—worshiping, walking, serving together—forgiving one another for what has hurt and divided you for centuries? Even men and women treat each other as respected equals in your community! And you do that . . . how? I need that kind of healing in my life." If we took Jesus at his word, evangelism would no longer be just about us pursuing the world one person at a time. *The world would come running to us.*

It's not rocket science. It's the Kingdom of God. So why aren't we about it? Why do we continue to treat church like a religious club of clones instead of a supernatural, redemptive community shouting to the world, "Jesus is here! Our healing has begun!" One reason: the intensity of this battle front. Satan knows that if he loses here, he's done. If the church becomes one, the world will know beyond doubt that Jesus comes from God—so Satan deploys every weapon in hell's arsenal to perpetuate division. And our battle strategy in response is . . . anemic. Typical, "just do it" Christianity—a few prayer meetings and sermon series, sprinkled with a little guilt and a plea to try harder, before we retreat to divided, separated, disheartening, spiritually lifeless normal. The world is choking and drowning in the blood of severed relationships and desperately scouring the landscape for some sign of hope, and when they see us, they see . . . nothing. Trust me, they hear our rhetoric about healing, forgiveness, restoration, and a love that conquers all, but they see *nothing.*

Maybe we ignore Jesus' command to come together because we don't trust him and his love enough—or at least not as much as we trust whatever strategy we found the last time we Googled evangelism. Maybe we don't love lost folks enough; loving and worshiping with those who aren't like us may cost us more than we're willing to pay. Or maybe, most frightening of all, we just don't love Jesus enough—at least not more than we love our comfortable enclaves of half-baked Christianity. But this I know: Whenever we get serious about Jesus' command to love one another with his sacrificial love, hell retreats.

In the summer of 1996, a Ku Klux Klan rally took place in Ann Arbor, Michigan. Eighteen-year-old Keshia Thomas was walking toward a woman with a bullhorn who was talking passionately to a group of counterprotesters about injustice when suddenly the woman shouted, "There's a Klansman in the crowd; get him!" The crowd quickly turned toward a man wearing a Confederate flag T-shirt. As Keisha ran toward the group, she saw someone hit him with a sign. He fell to the ground, and the people around him started kicking him in the head. Without hesitation, Keshia did the unthinkable: She threw her body over this man who hated her simply because of the color of her skin, protecting him from the blows. Later, Keshia said, "It felt like two angels had lifted my body and laid me down."[7]

The impact was instantaneous. "It felt like love and hope shot through the crowd," Keshia remembers, folks from both sides holding up their hands to keep the rest of the crowd back.[8] Twenty years later, the Klansman's son reached out to Keshia on Facebook. They got together, and he told her that against all odds, he had rejected his father's racist views. But that's not all. Keshia, African American daughter of God, and this son of a white supremacist traveled together to Flint, Michigan, where they stood side by side to bring healing to those affected by the city's deadly water crisis.

Without the name of Jesus Christ ever being mentioned, Jesus' love saved a hateful man's life—and later, saved the man's son from a life of hate. Then, Jesus' love took Keshia and her new brother to a struggling city where together, they pushed back the darkness. No seminars, sermons, or new legislation—just the powerful love of Jesus Christ overcoming hell's divisive agenda in the lives of a son and daughter of God. A living picture of Jesus' vision for his church.

Sometimes I think the kind of unity Jesus prayed for is never going to happen. Then I think of Jesus, bloody and broken, and remember, *This is why he died.* This is "thy kingdom come, thy will be done on earth as it is in heaven." So if you're serious about living into Jesus' prayer for us to be a living, collective witness of his love, here's some boots-on-the-ground insight into loving a brother or sister in Christ—even an enemy—in a way that *will not fail* to bring us together:

> Finally, all of you be of one mind, having compassion for
> one another.
> I PETER 3:8

The word *compassion* might be more clearly translated as "to feel with."[9] *The first step in moving toward another believer, even if we feel uncomfortable or they have hurt us, is to "feel with" them.* This isn't easy. Shame, insecurity, and self-centeredness often keep us locked down in our own story, unable to hear or *feel with* others in theirs. But Jesus' love frees us to be truly present to another. So, secured in his love, sit with your brother or sister, putting aside your agenda, your narrative, your judgment and ideas about who they are and what they believe—as well as your fear and need to control. Surrender all of it, in his name, and simply listen. Ask Jesus to help you let go of your addiction to thoughts, concepts, and ideology—and *feel with* the other person's heart, experience, and life. And then watch what the Holy Spirit does.

First, you'll find that in some ways, you have misjudged them. Some of the reasons you were angry or afraid or kept your distance from a brother or sister turn out to be divisive lies of the enemy! You'll also find yourself growing to love and accept them because you realize in so many ways—*you are them.* Loneliness, pain, grief, laughter, joy, and hope don't know color, gender, class, age, or denomination. They are God-given emotions that connect us—all of us—in a bond not easily broken.

Last year, after a retreat session, I was honored to listen to a sister pour out her heart about wounds she had received from men over the years. She talked and wept, and I listened . . . and then asked questions and listened some more. I analyzed nothing. Instead, I absorbed her pain and then poured out her wounds to the Father through my own tears, begging him to heal her past and give hope to her future. Later, she shared with a friend, "For the first time in my life, I felt like a man actually heard me and defended me. I felt so safe and supported. I will remember his prayer for me always." By the way, this sister in Christ is Korean American, and I'm old enough to be her father. When we feel with one another—culture, age, gender, or any other potential division takes a back seat. The love of God connects our hearts in a bond the enemy cannot sever.

So, my white brother, what if you sit down with a brother of color, listen to his story, and allow your heart to simply *feel with* him? Of course, brother of color, then turn in love and *feel with* your white brother. But I'm purposely starting with a white brother as "listener" because historically, white believers have often assumed that their narrative is the correct one—even the only one. Jesus can't unify his church until we stop trying to love from a position of control. Men, sit with your sisters in Christ—friends, wives, daughters, mothers— and *feel with* them the joys and sorrows of being a woman in today's world. Sisters, in love, do the same with your brothers, husbands, fathers, and friends. If you have resources, *feel with* the story of a brother or sister who has little. Sit with someone who wrestles with depression, chronic illness, or sexuality and *feel with* their hopes, fears, victories, and defeats. *Compassionate listening releases the love of Jesus to heal what Satan has torn apart.* When we *feel with* one another, the Holy Spirit begins to heal division and make us one—proving that Jesus comes from God and showcasing the good news of his powerful love to our relationally fractured world.

When the love of Jesus Christ moves us to *feel with* a brother or sister, and we allow our hearts to be deeply impacted by their pain of experienced injustice, *we will be moved to action on their behalf.* I fight for equality for women in culture and the body of Christ because I've felt the pain of my three daughters fighting to feel valued in a world still dominated by men. If you allow your heart to feel my brothers William and Alan as they weep over their family members who were lynched—as well as the injustice they experience today—nothing could keep you from marching for racial justice. The same is true for the lives of unborn babies, inequities facing the poor—and so much more. We're commanded to display Jesus' gospel to our broken world through "good works" (1 Peter 2:11-12)—not just in our private moral life but through bold acts of justice and mercy in his name. In the aftermath of the tragic, unjust killings of George Floyd, Ahmaud Arbery, and Breonna Taylor, two resolute agnostics I know of moved toward our God because of the strong action taken by followers of Jesus for racial justice and equality—in other words, evangelism. On the other hand—*when the church doesn't stand for justice, the world scoffs.* Not only at us, but at Jesus himself.

One final love story. Bethesta King was a gifted, passionate, hilarious, sometimes belligerent, extremely intelligent—and deeply wounded—forty-five-year-old man who used to hang out, day after day, on the porch of Hope Community Church. He was usually dead drunk and often reeked of urine. Nevertheless, King always wanted to talk religion—and would argue loudly and often convincingly the counterpoint of any piece of Jesus' good news you tried to share, for hours. Then, one day . . . King was gone. Sue,[10] Monique, and I, three of Hope's employees, had spent hours with King on the porch. We loved him and missed him dearly—and had no idea where he went until a few years later, when he showed up for church one Sunday. King's eyes were bright and clear. He had put on some weight. But the biggest tell that something had changed was that he sat on the front row, brandishing a genuine smile. Sue and I both saw him—but it wasn't until the end of the service, when our community joined hands in the middle of the sanctuary, that I mouthed, *It's good to see you again, my brother*—and Sue literally climbed over pews to get to her friend after the closing "amen." They stood and embraced for a very long time.

King told me a few weeks later that when he left Hope's porch, he wandered to another part of our neighborhood and set up camp in an abandoned house. One morning, he woke up shivering; it was so cold, his beer had frozen. He said, "I thought about you guys at Hope and how you loved me all those years and then felt God saying to me, *If you don't stop, son, you're going to die.* So, Pastor Kevin, I got clean. Got a job working at a halfway house. Got a car. And decided one Sunday, it was time for me to come back home."

I baptized King on May 8, 2016. Before he got in the pool, he shared, "It was the love you all showed me that brought me to my senses." Then he added, "Even when I was, you know, stinkin', angry, and lost." When King came up out of the water, he let out a whoop and holler unlike anything I'd ever heard before! He jumped out of the portable baptismal tank and, still wearing his waterlogged white robe, ran victory laps around the sanctuary like he had just scored a last-second, winning touchdown in the Super Bowl. Life. Joy. Glory.

King moved into our men's transitional home and lived there for several months. Then, on the evening of December 17, 2016, I got a call that King had gone to be with Jesus. Stroke or heart attack— whatever it was only took him from this life. The love of Jesus took him home. A love shared through imperfect people who themselves had been redeemed by Christ's love. A powerful, freeing love of Jesus available to all of us . . . in the abiding life.

Chapter 11

ABIDING JOY

I have told you these things so that you will be filled with my joy.
Yes, your joy will overflow!

JOHN 15:11, NLT

Of all accusations against Christians, the most terrible one was uttered
by Nietzsche when he said that Christians had no joy. . . . 'For behold, I
bring you good tidings of great joy'—thus begins the Gospel, and its end
is: 'And they worshipped him and returned to Jerusalem with great joy.'
(Luke 2:10; 24:52). And we must recover the meaning of this great joy.

ALEXANDER SCHMEMANN

Abiding in Jesus' love is learning to receive
his joy in the midst of spiritual battle.

OUR CHURCH WAS NEW to the Jefferson Chalmers community, a historic, east-side Detroit neighborhood wrestling with drugs, crime, and economic challenge—but also home to some of the coolest folks I'd ever met. The church building we bought was ninety years old—and the porch, complete with awning and sturdy metal rail to lean against, was a favorite hangout for our community's young men. For the first few weeks after our arrival, my daily ritual included a regular exchange of head-nods and "hey, how's it going" whenever I entered our building.

One day, the guys had moved off the porch and were standing on the adjacent urban street corner talking, laughing—doing what guys do when they get together—and I decided to introduce myself more formally. I approached, stuck out my hand, and said, "My name is Kevin, and I'm the pastor of this church"—I pointed to our building—"and thought it might be good for us to meet."

So here I was, a middle-aged, middle-class, six-foot-two, 220-pound white guy—a pastor, no less, and new to a tough neighborhood—sauntering uninvited into a huddle of several young African American brothers as if we're old pals. Possibly uneventful, except for what happened next. One of the guys, Darryl, slowly extended his hand, and I grabbed it and pulled him in to a bear hug, like I do with everyone.

The street corner got quiet as Darryl's friends paused their conversation. I found out later that this was, to them, a very strange scene. When I pulled back, I looked Darryl in the eye and offered, "I'd love to get to know you, son. If you or the other guys ever want to talk—or if there's anything else I can do to serve you as an older brother, please let me know." I smiled, Darryl nodded, and that was it.

The next few years, I got to know Darryl and many other young men and women in our new community, partly through a group we started on Wednesday afternoons to talk about jobs, study the Bible, and eat pizza. Eventually, Darryl graduated from high school, left the neighborhood for a while (went to college, I think), and then, one Wednesday out of nowhere, showed back up at our group. Darryl was well-loved and missed—so the room went crazy and everyone ate, laughed, and talked for several minutes until Darryl finally turned toward me at the other end of the table. He said, "Hey pastor, remember that day when we met outside on the corner of Jefferson and Marlborough and you came right up and gave me that old man hug? I didn't know what to think—it was weird, pastor, because me and my friends, we didn't really hug like that, and besides, you're a white guy and we didn't even know you!" Darryl started laughing along with everyone else, including me. Then, the room got awkwardly quiet. I said, "I remember that day like it was yesterday, Darryl. Looking back, I get how strange that moment must have been for you. But, a question, son. How do you feel now?"

Without hesitation, Darryl looked me in the eye and said, "Oh, that's easy. We all know you love us."

That was ten years ago. But I can still vividly remember what I felt when Darryl spoke those words—and what I'm feeling now as I relive the story. *I felt joy.* Deep, exhilarating, overflowing joy that somehow, over the years, despite my awkwardness, my age, my whiteness—Darryl had grown to know that I love him. That's the reason I reached out across natural lines of division that day on the street corner. I didn't yet know those young men, but I loved them. Not because they were young or black or because I wanted anything from them—but because they were beloved sons of the Father, the same Father who loved me.

Listen carefully: The kind of love we try to produce through discipline and diligence will . . . not . . . work. Ever. It's manufactured, fake, powerless, unsustainable. "Love one another, *as I have loved you*," Jesus said, not because we try hard or stay up all night memorizing Bible verses about love but because when we experience his love, we're compelled to love others. Jesus' love overcomes "a multitude of sins" (1 Peter 4:8)—in this case, my awkwardness, the deep wounds of racism, age difference, peer-pressure, and fear. His love miraculously creates space for two of his children to really see each other, to be fully known and accepted (Genesis 2:25). And wherever the powerful, healing love of Jesus Christ is present—*so is his joy.*

This is exactly what Jesus promised:

As the Father has loved me, so have I loved you. Abide in my love. If you keep my commandments, you will abide in my love. . . . *These things I have spoken to you, that my joy may be in you, and that your joy may be full.*

This is my commandment, that you love one another, as I have loved you.

JOHN 15:9-12, ESV, EMPHASIS ADDED

Remember, in a solemn moment, only hours before being crucified, Jesus deputizes his disciples—and us—to go into the world and *be him*, battling the powers of darkness for the lives of God's sons and daughters. But there's more. The abiding life isn't simply about struggle, blood, tears, and sacrifice. Through the power of his love, Jesus promises *otherworldly joy*, even as shells explode overhead. Jesus calls us not only to a life of Kingdom battle empowered by his love—but also, against all odds, to a life surrounded by his joy!

But what exactly is this joy—which Jesus claims as his own and promises to give to us? First, and maybe most importantly, we need to differentiate between the joy of Jesus Christ and its distant cousin, the joy of this present world. Both have to do with feelings of happiness, delight, and great pleasure. But the joy of the world is dependent on circumstances going our way. If our health is good, we get paid, our favorite team wins, and we go out for ice cream afterward, we can honestly say, "I enjoyed my day!" There's nothing wrong with this kind of joy. In fact, it's a really good thing to laugh, party, and be wonderfully happy about the blessings of life. But at best, this joy is fleeting and inconsistent—because it's dependent on circumstances that, in a fallen world engaged in cosmic spiritual war, you simply can't depend on.

But the joy Jesus describes is steady and constant because it isn't necessarily connected to happy life moments. Instead, this kind of joy, according to Jesus' words, is a *deep relational gladness*—deeper even than life's pain—*flowing from the Father's love, to the Son, to us, and then to one another.* Stay connected to his love, and you'll stay connected to his joy.

This secure, uninterrupted relationship-joy connection begins with our personal, intimate love relationship with Jesus himself. Only one chapter later in the book of John, Jesus warns the disciples they will be devastated when he dies—but then quickly promises, "When I see you again, you'll be full of joy, and it will be *a joy no one can rob from you*" (John 16:23-24, MSG, emphasis added). His post-resurrection appearances would prove that his promise to come to them in the person of the Holy Spirit was true. He had beaten death. His disciples would be intimately connected to him forever in a relationship of abiding love, experiencing joy like a "river overflowing its banks!" (John 16:23-24, MSG). A joy that no one could steal, that no pain or devastation could touch. Wow.

My friends, the good news is this is our promise too. But here's the deal: Jesus' joy is attached to deep intimacy with him. If our relationship is shallow, all about rules, discipline, and performance, we won't experience his joy. All we'll know is the malaise of obligation and shame. We may hang in there for a time, but when spiritual attack comes our way, we'll run for the hills. Without his joy, the intensity of the battle with hell over God's sons and daughters will crush us. We'll either retreat to an addictive search for the shallow joy of "our best life now"—complete with feel-good Bible verses and Christian slogans and never taking a risk for God's Kingdom again. Or we'll drift away from Jesus altogether. When I got fired and later when Carla got cancer—both experiences of intense spiritual battle—I found myself looking for the exit. What I didn't realize was that Jesus was calling me to a deeper intimacy with him, a place where his joy lives and promises to cover me no matter what.

But if Jesus is our One Great Love—nothing, not even hell itself—can rob us of his joy. I'm reminded of an etching in a wall at Auschwitz, the most notorious of all the Nazi death camps, where a million innocents were slaughtered in World War II. In the death block where prisoners were held before being gassed, a Polish soldier, awaiting his own death, used his fingernails to scratch the Sacred Heart of Jesus—a well-known symbol of Jesus' relentless love for the world.[1] I can't know for sure what was going on in the heart of this innocent soldier during his final hours. I suspect he at least wrestled with anger, fear, and despair. But it seems nothing in his cell was stronger than the presence of Jesus' love. And where his love prevails, so does his joy—a deep gladness more powerful than the hate and bitterness which easily could have crushed this young martyr's spirit. *A tenacious, supernatural joy Jesus promises those who abide in his love.*

Still, to be honest: Joy doesn't come easily to me. When I told Carla that joy was the topic of the final chapter of this book, she teasingly quipped, "Short chapter, eh?" Because she knows I'm so much better at connecting with the world's ever-present wound than any kind of joy—especially the wonderful joy of the moment. A few years back, we were at a Detroit Pistons basketball game, and she could tell I was emotionally disconnected from the fun—no smiling, laughing, or shouting at fast-break dunks. I sheepishly explained, "Carla, I can't stop thinking about all the people in this arena, wondering if they know God loves them." Some of my connection to the world's pain is Jesus. Some is about the way I'm wired. But the rest—personal baggage.

I felt a lot of sadness as a child. My first memory of pure joy is blurry, but real. I was three or four. I met a little girl in our neighborhood—maybe a bit older than me—and we played house in her backyard. We made a tent, and she was the mommy and I was the daddy—typical kid stuff. But what made it special, and why the memory is so clear and powerful, is that she was so gentle and kind to me. I could tell she genuinely liked me and liked being around me—feelings I wasn't used to. I didn't know much about God yet, but looking back, I think it was the first time I felt his love for me, even before that winter evening in the church where I trusted Jesus. I know for sure it was the first time I felt joy. I wanted to stay there in that backyard tent, like Peter, James, and John begged to stay on the mountain where Jesus unveiled his glory. Because like that mountain experience with Jesus, our backyard-blanket playhouse was filled with so much joy . . . it felt like a true home, a place where I belonged.

Over four months into the pandemic, with all its anxiety, isolation, and loss—including the uphill battle to conquer racial injustice—I long for more of the joy Jesus promised. On a personal level, my medical issues persist, adding a layer of anxiety and isolation for both Carla and me, and we miss our girls and their families terribly. Some of us may come by joy easily. But most of us, though we might occasionally feel circumstantial happiness, find that experiencing Jesus' joy, which nothing can steal from us, is far more difficult. Two of the happiest brothers and sisters in Christ I know are struggling to find joy today because they both just lost sons. Our dear friends whose four-year-old is battling leukemia are so much fun, but today, they desperately need joy. Those of us longing for racial justice are searching for joy in the battle, right now, to see the whole gospel fully realized. Maybe you, too, in the midst of your own story, would be grateful to know more about how to *experience* the joy Jesus promises.

Here's what I know: I can't make myself feel joy . . . and neither can you. Paul says, "The fruit of the Spirit is . . . joy" (Galatians 5:22-23). In other words, only the Holy Spirit, working in partnership with Jesus, can birth joy in the pain. Indeed, sometimes, that's exactly what happens—in a moment when we should only feel the fear and anguish of life, of spiritual battle . . . instead, we feel his joy! We can't explain it. It's a gift. We receive it, and we keep on walking—thankfully—with the Jesus who gave it. Gratitude is joy's inseparable partner. Thankfulness flows naturally when we experience Jesus' joy (Psalm 95:1-2; 1 Thessalonians 5:16-18).

But other times, when the battle is especially bloody and intense, we must fight for joy—because the powers of darkness are constantly warring to keep us from experiencing it. The question is: How do we fight for joy?

"Just do it" Christianity relentlessly beckons us to try harder. One prominent Christian leader recommends that we read three Bible verses on joy every morning until we start to feel joyful. No offense, but that's nonsense. At least, that kind of programmatic approach has never worked for me and has always resulted in further frustration, sadness, and shame. Besides, as we've talked about throughout this book, I'm not looking for Christian behavior modification, and I don't think you are either. We long for supernatural transformation. So, today, as I fight hell for the joy I desperately need but struggle to feel, I'm looking to the Jesus who loves me . . . to give me his promised joy: "Lord, on many levels, my spirit is struggling. I'm not asking you to take me *out* of the battle but to give me your joy to strengthen and sustain me *in* the battle. Please, Lord. Your joy. In the darkness. Please."

And then . . . I wait. Waiting is often a pathway to the joy we long for. But waiting is hard. Real hard. In fact, waiting is one of the disciplines of the abiding life because waiting doesn't come naturally.

Instead, waiting calls us to *choose* to trust that Jesus really loves us; that he is with us, feeling our pain and hearing our cry; and that he will answer. We must *choose* to stay present where Jesus has us in the moment instead of running away, addictively searching for instant relief. Sometimes waiting is difficult simply because when we think we ought to be doing something, we feel like we're doing nothing. But Sue Monk Kidd says convincingly,

> When you're waiting, you're *not* doing nothing. You're doing the most important something there is. You're allowing your soul to grow up.[2]

Lamentations describes this difficult growing-up process. In one of the most painful moments in Israel's history—Jerusalem under siege, her citizens starving in her streets, all hope lost—the prophet Jeremiah says,

> The LORD is good to those who *wait* for him. . . .
> It is good that one should *wait* quietly
>   for the salvation of the LORD.
>
> LAMENTATIONS 3:25-26, ESV, EMPHASIS ADDED

Unbelievable. Yet into this darkness—as Israel waits and as we wait for the One who is our only hope—Jeremiah speaks some of the most powerful, encouraging words in all of history:

> The steadfast love of the LORD never ceases;
>   his mercies never come to an end;
> they are new every morning;
>   great is your faithfulness.
>
> LAMENTATIONS 3:22-23, ESV

Forty-three years ago, Carla and I sang these words at our wedding. Words we've found to be true. God has always, always eventually shown up with his steadfast love and mercies that never end. And so, in the darkness, trusting in his faithfulness, we abide in Jesus' love—and wait for joy.

But remember: Joy, like peace, isn't a spiritual commodity Jesus gives apart from himself. He is our peace. He is our joy. So, waiting for joy is waiting for the Jesus we trust is with us *to make his presence known in a way that brings a gladness deeper than the pain.* In other words, *joy arrives when we experience Jesus with us in the darkness.* And because he loves each of us individually, the way he comes to us will often be graciously customized to meet our exact need in the moment.

Twenty-seven years ago, on a July evening, Carla's dad was killed by a drunk driver. I'll never forget the moment we heard, "Carla, this is your mom. There's been an accident. Your dad didn't make it." Carla crumbled in my arms sobbing, "I don't have a dad; I don't have a dad." Losing her father began a long, dark night for my best friend. Month after month, Carla cried out to Jesus for his presence, his love—and his joy in her grief. And she waited. One cold, snowy Detroit day, she looked out the window of our home and saw . . . a robin. Immediately, she knew—*Jesus is here.* Every year since she was a little girl, Carla and her dad had a contest—who would see the first robin in the spring? The loser would buy the winner a hot-fudge sundae! It was one of Carla's most cherished memories with her father, so when she saw this robin in the dead of winter—she not only knew Jesus was present but that he understood and valued this special detail of her relationship with her dad. She wept. Yes, tears of sadness. But for the first time since her dad's death, also tears of deep joy. It was a turning point in her healing.

When you ask Jesus to reveal himself and his joy, live

expectantly—heart open, eyes peeled. Noah knew God's encouraging presence through a leaf-bearing dove. Moses heard God in a burning bush. The children of Israel experienced God in a pillar of fire, and Elijah through food delivered by ravens and later through "the sound of a gentle whisper" (1 Kings 19:12, NLT). The Holy Spirit appeared as a dove at Jesus' baptism, and Paul heard and saw Jesus in timely visions. Jesus will show up for you, too. He may make himself known through a passage of Scripture, a relationship, a dream, his creation— or something even more unique. But he *will* show up because he's faithful. And remember the most important truth of the abiding life: He'll show up because he loves us.

Lest some of us get discouraged that we're not feeling his joy like we "should," sometimes the joy of Jesus isn't at all like an amazing, ear-to-ear smile, a deep gladness that eradicates our pain in the moment. When David says, "Weeping may endure for a night, but joy comes in the morning" (Psalm 30:5), we often think that means that when the weeping is done, joy is free to take over. It would be great if life were that linear—but it's not. More often, especially in the bloodiest, most intense hours of battle, in the face of the greatest loss, Jesus' joy is mixed with our grief, fear, and pain.

Jesus spoke joy to Carla's heart—and her spirit lifted. She knew it was him, and it changed everything. But she also continued to weep over her dad. She still lived in anguish over not being able to say good-bye, our girls missing their granddad, and why her loving father had to die at the hands of a man with thirty empties in the back of his truck. But, as Paul says, we grieve, but not as those who "have no hope" (1 Thessalonians 4:13). *Joy is mixed with sorrow but not overcome by sorrow.* Because Jesus and his joy are deeper than the sorrow. That's what Jesus promised. Stay connected to his love, stay connected to his joy. A joy no one can steal. All the way home.

We cannot miss one more extremely important aspect of this deep gladness: According to Jesus, his joy flows from the Father's love, to the Son, to us—*and then from us, to one another.* Our experience of joy is grounded in our personal, intimate relationship with Jesus himself but is also experienced in and through the love we share with all the others he loves.

"I love you and long to see you, dear friends, *for you are my joy,*" Paul writes to the Philippian church (Philippians 4:1, NLT, emphasis added). Again, to his brothers and sisters in Thessalonica, "Yes, you are our pride and *joy*" (1 Thessalonians 2:20, NLT, emphasis added). In other words, the joy Jesus promised isn't about our joyful connection with him in isolation, but in his community. Are we surprised? We're created in the image of a God who has experienced joy in himself—Father, Son, Holy Spirit—from all eternity. How could our relationships with one another, grounded in his Trinitarian love, not be a primary source of his joy?

Yes, many relationships bring us circumstantial happiness. Golfing buddies, fellow soccer parents, friendly neighbors, family that shows up for holidays. It's all good, as far as it goes. But the truth is, any of these relationships can explode into a million bloody fragments at any time—because often they are shallow, tentative, and based on performance, surface similarities, the mood of the moment, and what's-in-it-for-me attitude. These relationships bring us a happiness of sorts—until they don't. But they can't bring us deep joy.

Unfortunately, this is true even in the body of Christ. Carla and I have lost many "close Christian friends" over the years due to various theological differences, political preferences, or because we were no longer convenient. Many of you have experienced this kind of shallowness as well. Here's the deal: If our relationships are grounded in the shallows, they will eventually bring us heartache. In the heat of battle, shallowness cannot survive. Only when our relationships are rooted in the powerful, abiding love of Jesus Christ will we find the secure, lasting relational joy we long for.

Carla, daughter of God, precious friend, love of my life—*you are my joy*. Andrea, Leigh Anne, Caroline—my little girls but also my grown-up sisters in Christ—each of you, in your own extraordinary way, are my joy. Dusty and John, not just sons-in-law but sons and my brothers in Christ—you are my joy. Ada, Mack, Van, little Johnny—so young in God's great Kingdom, but you've already taught me so much about the love of Jesus—you are my joy! My closest brothers and sisters in Christ over the last forty years (you know who you are): Together we have taken the risk to know and be known and have found deep, lasting love, acceptance, and intimacy in Jesus Christ. We've fought together for the lives of those God loves so much, and each of you, more than you will ever know, are my great joy.

Without the joy of each of these deep relationships where I have been known, loved, accepted, and cherished—no matter the cost—I would have long ago abandoned my Christian faith. I say this not to shock or offend you but to make sure you understand that these joy-producing relationships aren't optional but crucial to the abiding life. I wasn't meant to survive without them. Neither are you. I know joy-filled, covenant relationships are difficult to find. But this I also know: Deep calls to deep. Start by falling more deeply in love with Jesus. Then look around you—there might be others longing for the same deep, relational joy but waiting for someone else to take the first step. Eleven years ago, I asked a dozen men if they'd be willing to journey with me toward intimacy in Jesus. We walk together still, and each of them are my joy. Perhaps it can be the same for you.

The love of Jesus is so powerful that sometimes a joy-filled connection can be a glance, a touch, a simple, profound moment. Whenever two people risk being known—followed by love and acceptance—joy is birthed quickly, powerfully, miraculously, bringing light to the darkness.

Like the wounded young man I met at a retreat a few years ago, who didn't believe in Jesus or God or much of anything but trying to survive. We sat for a couple of hours one afternoon, and I simply listened, felt his pain, held his hands in mine, and gently spoke the love of Jesus. The next morning, he called me aside and whispered, "Yesterday, I prayed for the first time in my life." My brother, wherever you are, you are my joy.

Or Annie—a dynamic, courageous young mom and recovering addict with deep wounds who allowed me and her pastor to pray over her one Sunday afternoon. Annie sobbed out her pain as we spoke words of healing fatherly love. She said later, "That moment was an awakening. I'll never be the same." Bless you, daughter of God. You are my joy.

Or the little boy I never met who one day filled out a church welcome card I've hung onto for decades. His words: "I love God yes you God plese make me live with my daddy." I honor your faith, son, and pray God answered the cry of your heart. For many years, you have been my joy.

My friends, keep your heart open and eyes peeled. As you choose to abide in Jesus' love, you, too, will see and experience his joy in others—everywhere. And when you step into glory, you'll be greeted by countless sons and daughters of God, who, one at a time, approach you and passionately declare, "In the darkness, *you* . . . were my joy."

I wonder how the nonbelieving world would respond to two billion followers of Jesus Christ experiencing his joy in the darkness. What if we exchanged the fake smiles and forced optimism of "just do it" Christianity for the deep gladness of Jesus, shouting to the world, "The light shines in the darkness, and the darkness has not overcome it" (John 1:5, ESV). United Pursuit sings, "You're taking me by the hand again / Giving me strength to dance again / Cause your love changes everything."[3] Dancing for joy—in the darkness, with our One Great Love. A picture of the abiding life.

Epilogue

FREE INDEED

If the Son sets you free, you will be free indeed.

JOHN 8:36, ESV

FREEDOM. The longing, birthright, and lifeblood of every son and daughter of God ever born. Physical freedom, for sure. But also freedom of the spirit. Freedom in our walk with the Jesus who lived and died to set us free.

And yet—for too long, so many of us have lived under the shaming, finger-pointing glare of a false god, in the miserable shackles of a "just do it" Christianity that told us if we just knew more and tried harder, we would finally be able to successfully walk with Jesus. As you already know, that was my story. I grew up learning to manage my Christian journey through a combination of rigid theological categories, well-defined rules, self-discipline, and rigorous study. Then one day, God mercifully allowed my seemingly well-put-together life to fall apart, revealing a hidden brokenness that was crying out for healing . . . and freedom.

Just six months after our wedding, Carla and I had a bad argument one evening . . . and I lost it. For the first and only time in our marriage, I inexcusably put my hands on the love of my life. In a rage I didn't understand, I shoved her—and she ended up on the living-room floor of our ten-by-forty-foot mobile home—looking up at me with hurt and shock. The crazy thing is, I knew better than most what the Bible says about love and respect in marriage. I could have quoted Ephesians 5:25, "Husbands, love your wives, just as Christ also loved the church" in New Testament Greek, in the middle of our argument! But here's what I didn't understand: No matter how spiritually together or self-disciplined we think we are, the power of *damaged emotions will trump cognitive truth*, every time.

Later, I realized the overwhelming rage I felt in that moment wasn't about "that moment" but about the trauma of an angry, shame-based childhood. That truth didn't excuse my behavior—at all. But it was a severe mercy that helped me realize the days of "managing" my Christian experience were over. No amount of rebuking the rage or denying my childhood trauma would make me whole. I needed God to do something in me that was beyond my understanding. Jesus calls it healing. Paul calls it *transformation*:

> And all of us . . . seeing the glory of the Lord as though reflected in a mirror, *are being transformed* into the same image from one degree of glory to another; for this comes from the Lord, the Spirit.
>
> 2 CORINTHIANS 3:18, NRSV, EMPHASIS ADDED

Transformation means change. Change we don't make happen—but happens *to us*, by the power of the Spirit. Change happening right now, whether we feel it or not. Change available to all of us, no matter how broken or irreligious.

Are you getting this? We settle for "growth in Christ" that is shallow and surface—the keeping of a few pet Christian rules, explained with self-congratulatory words like *discipline* and *commitment*. Listen, if we can explain our growth in Christ—it really isn't growth in Christ at all. Of course, we can give our wounds and sin a coat of fresh try-harder paint. But only God can transform our dust—into glory.

Thankfully, after I spent hours weeping, praying, and repenting, Carla graciously forgave me. That night, I began letting go of "just do it" Christianity's shallow, powerless system of behavior modification dressed up as sanctification—and took my first step toward the real Jesus and the freedom he offers. The next morning, I went alone to church and asked an elder to pray over me. I didn't tell him how jacked up I was, but I told the Lord, "Jesus, I don't know what to do, but I know I need deliverance that I can't give myself. Please show me the way." The very next day, I was in the office of a Christian counselor, beginning the mysterious process of healing—of being transformed into the image of Christ. I've already described the many halting stops and starts of the next thirteen years, culminating in my final break with shame-based religion after my near suicide. But I never went fully back to the old, worthless try-harder system after that broken evening with my dearest friend, Carla, in our newlywed mobile home.

The journey to freedom is slow and deliberate. But it's also deep and real. Am I completely transformed today? No. But when I relapse and act out in sin—what I never, ever do is double down on trying to get my act together. When Jesus makes me aware of my wandering— I run to him. My Healer. My One Great Love. On Father's Day this year, Carla signed her card to me, "I couldn't love or respect you more." Unbelievable. I was an out-of-control rageaholic. My wife was ready to leave me. Today, she loves, respects, and trusts me because she sees my transformation that has nothing to do with Christianized effort but can only be explained by the unexplainable power of Jesus' love to heal a broken man's life.

I want this freedom so badly for you that I'm choked up as I write these words. Whatever you struggle with, wherever you find yourself locked down, Jesus Christ longs to set you free. *But you must surrender to his healing and transformation.* You must let go of the trying and striving and explaining and controlling—and cry out in desperation at Jesus' feet, "I can't. You must. I'm yours. Show me the way."

Right now, Jesus himself is very near. He sees the real you—how weary you are after years of laboring, performing, and striving to keep all the rules, to do the right thing, to be a "good Christian." His eyes, lovingly focused on you, are full of compassion, not disappointment. Encouragement, not criticism. Acceptance, not demand.

Can you hear his gentle voice? "I love you so much, daughter. I've always loved you, son. It's time to lay your burden down. I'm the One your heart has been desperately longing for. I am your One Great Love. I'm calling you to make your home in my love—to talk with me day and night about everything. To learn to listen to my loving, guiding voice through my Word and your heart. To connect in authentic, life-giving, healing relationships in my name. I'm asking you to trust my love enough to surrender your life to me—one moment at a time—even in the mystery and suffering of the battle. To allow my love to heal you from the wounds of shame and sin and launch you with undying compassion and great power into a broken world desperate for my love. Never forget: I'm with you, and I will never leave you. Ever. I am the resurrected One. I've conquered death. Even when hell is at your doorstep, there's no need to fear. Even then, you can know my peace and joy. Because I'm right by your side. So take my hand, son. Let's walk together, daughter. Not just today, but all the way home . . . to glory."

Freedom is here. His name is Jesus. He loves you. What are you waiting for? It's time.

Notes

INTRODUCTION: YOU CAN'T STOP LOVE

1. David Crowder, "Golgotha Hill (King of Love)," *I Know a Ghost* © 2018 sixstepsrecords.
2. Love Song, "Feel the Love," *Love Song* © 1971 Good News Records.
3. JG Abbot, "Remain," in *The Anchor Bible 29A: The Gospel According to John* (Garden City, NY: Doubleday, 1970), 663.
4. William F. Arndt and F. Wilbur Gingrich, *A Greek–English Lexicon of the New Testament and Other Early Christian Literature*, 4th ed., trans. and adapt. of Walter Bauer's German (Chicago: University of Chicago Press, 1957), 504–05.
5. N. T. Wright, *The Day the Revolution Began: Reconsidering the Meaning of Jesus's Crucifixion* (New York: HarperOne, 2018), 391, 403.
6. Used with permission.

CHAPTER 1: OUR ONE GREAT LOVE

1. For more on Sophia's story, see J. Kevin Butcher, *Choose and Choose Again: The Brave Act of Returning to God's Love* (Colorado Springs: NavPress, 2016), chap. 5.
2. Gregory A. Boyd, *Repenting of Religion: Turning from Judgment to the Love of God* (Grand Rapids, MI: BakerBooks, 2004), chap. 4.
3. Hans Urs von Balthasar, *Love Alone Is Credible*, trans. D. C. Schindler (San Francisco: Ignatius Press, 2004), preface.
4. Catherine of Siena, from her poem entitled "My Nature Is Fire."
5. See, for example, Randy Alcorn, "Is Genesis 3:8 Sufficient to Establish that God Was in the Habit of Visiting with Adam and Eve in the Garden?" Eternal Perspective Ministries, March 29, 2010, https://www.epm.org/resources/2010/Mar/29/gen-38-sufficient-establish-god-was-habit-visiting/.
6. Kallistos Ware, *The Orthodox Way*, rev. ed. (Crestwood, NY: St Vladimir's Seminary Press, 1995), 81.
7. United Pursuit, "Simple Gospel," *Simple Gospel* © 2015 United Pursuit.

CHAPTER 2: DESPERATION

1. Jesse Carey, "15 Augustine Quotes that Helped Shape Modern Christian Thought," *Relevant*, August 28, 2014, https://relevantmagazine.com/faith/15-augustine-quotes-helped-shape-modern-christian-thought/.
2. See her poem entitled "My Nature Is Fire."
3. Susan Bergman, "Twentieth-Century Martyrs: A Meditation," in *Martyrs: Contemporary Writers on Modern Lives of Faith*, ed. Susan Bergman (Maryknoll, NY: Orbis Books, 1998), 2.
4. Mary E. DeMuth, *Thin Places: A Memoir* (Grand Rapids, MI: Zondervan, 2010), 213. Emphasis added.
5. George MacDonald, "The Voice of Job," accessed October 1, 2020, http://www.online-literature.com/george-macdonald/unspoken-sermons/22/.
6. As quoted here: "A Quote by St. Porphyrios," *Hagia Sophia* (blog), April 15, 2018, https://orthodoxyhasguts.wordpress.com/2018/04/15/a-quote-by-st-porphyrios/.
7. Saint John of the Cross, *Dark Night of the Soul*, trans. E. Allison Peers (New York: Image Books, 1959), chap. XI, scanned in 1994, http://www.carmelitemonks.org/Vocation/DarkNight-StJohnoftheCross.pdf.
8. Frederick Buechner, *A Crazy, Holy Grace: The Healing Power of Pain and Memory* (Grand Rapids, MI: Zondervan, 2017), chap. 2.

CHAPTER 3: LONGING FOR HEALING

1. Jesus is reading from Isaiah 61. Emphasis added.
2. Terry Wardle, "The Formational Prayer Seminar" (The Institute of Formational Prayer, Ashland, Ohio, January 10–13, 2006).
3. Gregory A. Boyd, *Repenting of Religion: Turning from Judgment to the Love of God* (Grand Rapids, MI: BakerBooks, 2004), chap. 7–8.
4. Boyd, *Repenting*, 17, 92.
5. Quoted in Boyd, *Repenting*, 157.
6. Joshua Hawley, "The Age of Pelagius" *Christianity Today*, June 4, 2019, https://www.christianitytoday.com/ct/2019/june-web-only/age-of-pelagius-joshua-hawley.html.
7. N. T. Wright, *Advent for Everyone: A Journey with the Apostles* (Louisville, KY: Westminster John Knox Press, 2017), 15.
8. As quoted in Michael L. Brown, *Israel's Divine Healer* (Grand Rapids, MI: Zondervan, 1995), 197. Emphasis added.
9. Motyer, as quoted in Brown, *Israel's Divine Healer*, 197.
10. Matthew was quoting Isaiah 53:4 here.
11. Shared with permission from hymn's author.

CHAPTER 4: SURRENDER

1. J. Kevin Butcher, "Settling for a Fix-it God," *Covenant Companion*, March/April 2018, 51–53.

2. Buechner, *Crazy*, 41.
3. Bekah DiFelice, *Almost There: Searching for Home in a Life on the Move* (Colorado Springs: NavPress, 2017), 70.
4. Ibid.
5. Frederick Buechner, *The Sacred Journey: A Memoir of Early Days* (New York: HarperSanFrancisco, 1982), 46.
6. Julian of Norwich, *Revelations of Divine Love* (New York: Penguin Books, 1998), 175. Emphasis added.
7. Michael A. Hayes and David Tombs, eds., *Truth and Memory: The Church and Human Rights in El Salvador and Guatemala* (Herefordshire: Gracewing, 2001), 48.
8. Andrew Del Rossi, "A New Mural at Romero Center Ministries," Romero Center Ministries, September 2019, http://romero-center.org/st-oscar-romero-presentations/.

CHAPTER 5: WITH ME

1. Raymond E. Brown, *The Gospel According to John, XIII–XXI*, Anchor Bible (Garden City, NY: Doubleday, 1970), 642, 646.
2. N. T. Wright, *Simply Jesus: A New Vision of Who He Was, What He Did, and Why He Matters* (New York: HarperOne, 2011), 195–197; and N. T. Wright, *The Resurrection of the Son of God*, Christian Origins and the Question of God, vol. 3 (Minneapolis: Fortress Press, 2003), 655.
3. Fritz Rienecker and Cleon Rogers, *A Linguistic Key to the Greek New Testament* (Grand Rapids, MI: Zondervan, 1976), 560. Rienecker and Rogers suggest that the Greek word translated 'near' "could imply 'near in space' or 'near in time'. I'm convinced of the former rendition.
4. Leon Morris, *The Gospel According to John*, The New International Commentary on the New Testament (Grand Rapids, MI: Eerdmans, 1971), 653.
5. C. S. Lewis, *Prince Caspian* (New York: Collier Books, 1970), 132.
6. For more on Cindy's story, see J. Kevin Butcher, *Choose and Choose Again: The Brave Act of Returning to God's Love* (Colorado Springs: NavPress, 2016), chap. 9.
7. Eric Clapton, "Presence of the Lord," performed by Lizz Wright, *Fellowship* © 2010 Verve Forecast.
8. Henri J. M. Nouwen, *A Cry for Mercy: Prayers from the Genesee* (New York: Image Books, 2002), 20–21.

CHAPTER 6: MYSTERY AND THE LOVE OF JESUS

1. As quoted in Woodrow Kroll, *An Interview with God: Questions You're Asking and How the Bible Answers Them* (Chicago: Moody, 2004), epilogue.
2. Friedrich Nietzsche, *Twilight of the Idols* and *The Anti-Christ*, trans. R. J. Hollingdale (New York: Penguin Books, 2003), 137.
3. Frederick Buechner, *Telling Secrets: A Memoir* (New York: HarperCollins, 1991), 103.
4. Adrian Gibbs (DirtyRottenOversharerGibbs), Twitter, July 5, 2020, https://twitter.com/adriangibbs_/status/1279807721496289288.

5. Frederick Buechner, *Godric: A Novel* (New York: HarperSanFrancisco, 1983), 142.

6. Aubrey Sampson, *The Louder Song: Listening for Hope in the Midst of Lament* (Colorado Springs: NavPress, 2019), 54. Emphasis added.

7. Sampson, *Louder Song*, 54.

8. Barbara Lazear Ascher, "Martyrs Among Us," in *Martyrs: Contemporary Writers on Modern Lives of Faith*, ed. Susan Bergman (Maryknoll, NY: Orbis Books, 1998), 315, 317.

9. Albert King, "Everybody Wants to Go to Heaven," *Everybody Wants to Go to Heaven* © 1971 Stax Records.

10. "I Serve a Risen Savior," by A. H. Ackley, 1933.

11. For example, in a letter to Sheldon Vanauken (dated December 23, 1950), Lewis wrote: "Notice how we are perpetually *surprised* at Time. ('How time flies! Fancy John being grown-up & married! I can hardly believe it!') In heaven's name, why? Unless, indeed, there is something in us which is *not* temporal."

12. From the African American spiritual "Give Me Jesus."

CHAPTER 7: ALONE WITH OUR LOVE

1. Craig Glickman, *Solomon's Song of Love: Let the Song of Songs Inspire Your Own Romantic Story* (West Monroe, LA: Howard Publishing, 2004), 175.

2. N. T. Wright, *Following Jesus: Biblical Reflections on Discipleship* (Grand Rapids, MI: Eerdmans, 2014), 94.

3. For more on Dan's story, see J. Kevin Butcher, *Choose and Choose Again: The Brave Act of Returning to God's Love* (Colorado Springs: NavPress, 2016), chap. 1.

4. Frederick Buechner, *The Faces of Jesus: A Life Story* (Brewster, MA: Paraclete Press, 2005), 79.

5. George MacDonald, "The Word of Jesus on Prayer," in *Unspoken Sermons* (New York: Cosimo Classics, 2007), 166.

6. Frederick Buechner, *The Magnificent Defeat* (New York: HarperSanFrancisco, 1985), 126.

CHAPTER 8: HEALING LOVE IN JESUS' COMMUNITY

1. Dr. Curt Thompson, New Canaan Society national conference (Omni Orlando Resort, Championsgate, Florida, March 1–3, 2019).

2. Ibid.

3. Hezekiah Walker, "I Need You to Survive," *Family Affair II: Live at Radio City Music Hall* © 2002 Verity Records.

4. Biblical authors use the image of a lion to describe both predator (Satan) and protector (Messiah). For more on this topic, see www.evangelical-times. org/19691/lions-in-the-bible.

5. Andrew B. McGowan, *Ancient Christian Worship: Early Church Practices in Social,*

Historical, and Theological Perspective (Grand Rapids, MI: Baker Academic, 2014), 72–77.

6. Allan Menzies, ed., *The Ante-Nicene Fathers: Translations of the Writings of the Fathers Down to A.D. 325*, vol. IX, 5th ed. (New York: Charles Scribner's Sons, 1906), 276–77.

7. For more on Samson's story, see J. Kevin Butcher, *Choose and Choose Again: The Brave Act of Returning to God's Love* (Colorado Springs: NavPress, 2016), chap. 4.

CHAPTER 9: HEALING FROM SHAME

1. Sandra D. Wilson, *Released from Shame: Moving Beyond the Pain of the Past*, rev. ed. (Downers Grove, IL: IVP Books, 2002), 23.

2. "Guilt tells me": Wilson, *Released from Shame*, 10. "Guilt is about" and "Guilt can be forgiven": I don't recall where I first encountered these helpful concepts, but I've been applying them for years.

3. Curt Thompson, *The Soul of Shame: Retelling the Stories We Believe about Ourselves* (Downers Grove, IL: IVP Books, 2015), 12, 22.

4. Allan N. Schore, *The Science of the Art of Psychotherapy* (New York: Norton, 2012), 383, 399; and Simon Books, "20 Things Unborn Baby Can Feel during Pregnancy (that Moms Should Know)," BabyGaga.com, May 3, 2019, https://www.babygaga.com/20-things-unborn-baby-can-feel-during-pregnancy-that-moms-should-know/.

5. Robert Karen, "Shame," *Atlantic Monthly* (February 1992): 40–70, http://www.empoweringpeople.net/shame/shame.html.

6. Fred Rogers, "It's You I Like," 1971.

7. In the last decade, Dr. Brené Brown has powerfully championed vulnerability as the central pathway to healing our shame. She explains that "Vulnerability is the birthplace of love, belonging, joy" (*Daring Greatly: How the Courage to Be Vulnerable Transforms the Way We Live, Love, Parent, and Lead* [New York: Avery, 2015], 34) and that "You either walk into your story and own your truth, or you live outside of your story, hustling for your worthiness" ("In You Must Go: Harnessing the Force by Owning Our Stories," blog, Mary 4, 2018, https://brenebrown.com/blog/2018/05/04/in-you-must-go-harnessing-the-force-by-owning-our-stories/)

CHAPTER 10: SHARING OUR GREAT LOVE WITH A BROKEN WORLD

1. Geoffrey William Bromiley, *The Theological Dictionary of the New Testament, Abridged in One Volume*, ed. Gerhard Kittel and Gerhard Friedrich, s.v. "euangelion," accessed on Logos, September 30, 2020.

2. Edward E. Hindson and Daniel R. Mitchell, eds., *Zondervan King James Version Commentary: New Testament* (Grand Rapids, MI: Zondervan, 2010), 89.

3. Tim MacBride, *To Aliens and Exiles: Preaching the New Testament as a*

Minority-Group Rhetoric in a Post-Christendom World (Eugene, OR: Cascade Books, 2020), 123.

4. Madeleine L'Engle, *Walking on Water: Reflections on Faith and Art* (New York: Convergent Books, 2016), 113.

5. Eric Hatfield, "How Many Christian Denominations Worldwide?" *The Way* (blog), November 23, 2012, https://the-way.info/2012/11/23/how-many -christian-denominations-worldwide/.

6. N. T. Wright, *Paul: In Fresh Perspective* (Minneapolis: Fortress Press, 2009), 165.

7. Jim Schaefer, "A Few Minutes with . . . Someone Who Chose Nonviolence," *Detroit Free Press*, updated July 16, 2016, https://www.freep.com/story/news /columnists/jim-schaefer/2016/07/09/ann-arbor-rally-keshia-thomas/86878664/.

8. Ibid.

9. Geoffrey William Bromiley, *The Theological Dictionary of the New Testament, Abridged in One Volume*, ed. Gerhard Kittel and Gerhard Friedrich, s.v. "sumpatheis," accessed on Logos, September 30, 2020.

10. For more on Sue's story, see J. Kevin Butcher, *Choose and Choose Again: The Brave Act of Returning to God's Love* (Colorado Springs: NavPress, 2016), chap. 14.

CHAPTER 11: ABIDING JOY

1. Kathy DeVico, "His Heart, Our Heart," Redwoods Monastery, June 19, 2020, https://www.redwoodsabbey.org/blog/post/sacred-heart-2020.

2. As quoted in Sue Monk Kidd, *When the Heart Waits: Spiritual Direction for Life's Sacred Questions* (New York: HarperOne, 2006), 22.

3. United Pursuit, "Your Love Changes Everything," *Simple Gospel* © 2015 United Pursuit Records.

Acknowledgments

My first book, *Choose and Choose Again*, detailed our urgent need to not just know about the love of God but to experience it and featured redemptive stories of people rescued from despair by that same love. This second book was birthed when my close friend Carol said, "I get it, Kev. But many of us long for *more* on exactly *how* to find our way through the deep wounds and shaming voices that shout, 'God doesn't love you.' Show us *how* to really know that he loves us and then *how* to live saturated in his love for a lifetime." Thanks, dearest sister, for challenging me to think even more deeply about Abba's love and to wrestle even more fully with the mystery of *how* to abide in his love—all the way home.

Thanks, Don Jacobson, for encouraging me to keep writing about God's love and for believing in this project early on. To the NavPress team: It's difficult to capture the depth of my appreciation for each of you. Don Pape, I remember sending you a paragraph on the power and freedom of abiding in Jesus' love and your reply touching me deeply. "Write the book," you said. "We all need to know more about abiding. In fact, *I need to know more*." Olivia, thank you for your extremely important administrative work and Elizabeth, for your incredibly thoughtful and meticulous attention to detail in the final edit. And Caitlyn, my respected sister and colleague—you did it again. You took my early, confused ramblings about God's love and reorganized them into something readable and compelling. Then, throughout the process of finishing, you consistently beckoned me back to my true voice. Most profoundly, in some very dark writing moments, your belief in me and in the book's message helped keep me going. *Free* carries the significant imprint of your gifts—but also your passion for Jesus and people. I am forever grateful.

Tyndale, your partnership and input (the fabulous cover!) have been invaluable. Ed Underwood, as a brother *and* fellow writer, thanks for being there with empathy and writing wisdom whenever I called. Susan Lubinski, without your organizational gifts in my life and ministry, I would be lost. Thanks for your behind-the-scenes efforts connecting with all those whose stories we are honored to tell. To my Rooted Ministries, Inc. board of directors, thanks for believing in my dream that *Free* could be an important, meaningful resource for pastors and churches struggling with the bondage of "just do it" Christianity. And a special thank you to those who consistently prayed. I felt you battling hell on my behalf all the way to the last sentence. I will never forget.

To my precious family. Dusty and John, thanks for reading early chapters and encouraging me along the way—not only as a writer but as your brother in Christ. But most of all, thanks for being passionate men of integrity who not only bring healing to our broken world but love my daughters and grandchildren so very well. Ada, Mack, Van, and Johnny: Your Papa loves you so much. I pray that one day you will feel God's love *for you* through my words in this book. To Carla, my life partner and best friend: For five solid months during COVID-19, you tenaciously stood beside me, listening patiently while I read countless paragraphs aloud and encouraging me when I wanted to quit. Without your passionate, faithful love, reminding me of God's love at every challenging turn, I promise you—this book would never have been finished. I will love and cherish you, dearest friend, till the end of time.

Finally, to Andrea, Leigh Anne, and Caroline. It has been the greatest honor of my life to be your father. Indeed, you are my heart. I dedicate this book about the wondrous, abiding love of Jesus to each of you, praying that somehow, my deep love for you will continue to point you . . . to his.

THE NAVIGATORS® STORY

— ◐ —

T HANK YOU for picking up this NavPress book! I hope it has been a blessing to you.

NavPress is a ministry of The Navigators. The Navigators began in the 1930s, when a young California lumberyard worker named Dawson Trotman was impacted by basic discipleship principles and felt called to teach those principles to others. He saw this mission as an echo of 2 Timothy 2:2: "And the things you have heard me say in the presence of many witnesses entrust to reliable people who will also be qualified to teach others" (NIV).

In 1933, Trotman and his friends began discipling members of the US Navy. By the end of World War II, thousands of men on ships and bases around the world were learning the principles of spiritual multiplication by the intentional, person-to-person teaching of God's Word.

After World War II, The Navigators expanded its relational ministry to include college campuses; local churches; the Glen Eyrie Conference Center and Eagle Lake Camps in Colorado Springs, Colorado; and neighborhood and citywide initiatives across the country and around the world.

Today, with more than 2,600 US staff members—and local ministries in more than 100 countries—The Navigators continues the transformational process of making disciples who make more disciples, advancing the Kingdom of God in a world that desperately needs the hope and salvation of Jesus Christ and the encouragement to grow deeper in relationship with Him.

NAVPRESS was created in 1975 to advance the calling of The Navigators by bringing biblically rooted and culturally relevant products to people who want to know and love Christ more deeply. In January 2014, NavPress entered an alliance with Tyndale House Publishers to strengthen and better position our rich content for the future. Through *THE MESSAGE* Bible and other resources, NavPress seeks to bring positive spiritual movement to people's lives.

If you're interested in learning more or becoming involved with The Navigators, go to www.navigators.org. For more discipleship content from The Navigators and NavPress authors, visit www.thediscoplemaker.org. May God bless you in your walk with Him!

NavPress

www.navpress.com

CP1308